I0044953

Social Viability

Founding Policy

Social Viability

Founding Policy

RICHARD LANDER

This book is intended for use by those who have a capacity for understanding the consequences of their actions, who have the willingness to be responsible for the things they do, who have a desire to improve their lives and their world, and who have the ability to change conditions. Anyone reading and applying the ideas and suggestions in this book does so at their own risk…

…but to everyone's benefit.

Copyright © 2008 Social Viability, Inc.

This work is licensed under the Creative Commons Attribution-Noncommercial-No Derivative Works 3.0 Unported License.
To view a copy of this license, visit http://creativecommons.org/licenses/by-nc-nd/3.0/ or send a letter to Creative Commons, 171 Second Street, Suite 300, San Francisco, California, 94105, USA.

You are free:
- **to Share** — *to copy, distribute and transmit the work*

Under the following conditions:
- **Attribution**. *You must attribute the work in the manner specified by the author or licensor (but not in any way that suggests that they endorse you or your use of the work).*
- **Noncommercial**. *You may not use this work for commercial purposes.*
- **No Derivative Works**. *You may not alter, transform, or build upon this work.*

Any of the above conditions can be waived if you get express written permission from the copyright holder.

www.socialviability.com

ISBN: 978-0-6152-3684-1

TABLE OF CONTENTS

Chapter 6: The Messenger

Chapter 7: Opportunity

INTRODUCTION

SOCIAL VIABILITY was born out of a recognition that our modern culture needs to change if it is to survive.

When you take a look at today's world, you don't have to look far to find wars and terrorism, poverty and famine, crime and homelessness, corruption and dishonesty. Seeing these things you may question the motives driving those that influence global affairs.

You should.

Bankers are looting your pockets with their perverted, criminal scams. They are protected by political actors that are in their employ by way of election campaign contributions and lobbying measures. Their minions are boxing you in with elaborate and deceitful legal systems. They are financing and encouraging industrial activity that is infecting our populace with sickness and stupidity. And they are lying to you through their information outlets in the media and educational institutions.

If you doubt that this is the case, I suggest you put off reading this book for now. Alternatively, I would suggest that you throw away your television, read some history, then go and take an honest, objective look at your world and where it's headed. Perhaps over time, as you study your surroundings in light of where mankind has been, you may be more inclined to see things from the viewpoint that this book was written from. This book is based on the premise that our current global culture is on the decline and that viability must be restored to our collective efforts or our civilization will go the way of so many others in history, and become just that: history.

From the Industrial Revolution we have inherited the capacity for high productivity and hence, high standards of living. It is time for social and economic development that will allow us to grow into this wherewithal we have found ourselves with. Our current culture could be said to be like a child playing with a gun. If our ability to handle ourselves effectively does not mature, we stand to shoot ourselves in the face with the technology we now posses.

We must improve the viability of our collective efforts or each of our individual selves will suffer the consequences.

It is all well and good to notice that we need to change our social course, and it is perfectly reasonable to demand that we improve our lot given the course we find ourselves on, but none of these things will provide hope. Hope will require a new course—a map and a new heading that leads somewhere better.

And that is what we are dealing with in Social Viability. We are dealing with a map out of the social fecklessness that is so prevalent. There is a way out of this social mess gathering about us. There is a way to avert the tyrannical conditions that certain wealthy psychopaths have planned for us. There are ways to organize our social interaction that reward the productive, encourage benevolence and readily generate prosperity for those that are willing to put in an honest day's work.

But it will need the participation and help of those that see what we face. And, unless you read past the 5th paragraph in disregard of my suggestions, that means you.

Social Viability: the name communicates the objective. It is a fraternal organization that supplies sound policy and effective systems for the operation of a viable society; one that will not fail, but which will prosper and grow and develop into a culture that we can be proud of again.

In each of the six chapters that follow, we will take up two main topics. The first topic of each chapter deals with: "The Problem." It addresses those things which are corrupting our societies and herding the most powerful nations on Earth toward terminal failure. You will notice regular reference to the volume of wealth that is being siphoned off by these sectors of society. By referencing these burdens, I hope to illustrate the degree of wealth and prosperity that can be enjoyed by a society not encumbered with such corrupt and malfunctioning institutions. It is important to recognize the severe and far-reaching repercussions of these economic burdens that are being carried by the working class. It drives many families into poverty, and the many more it drives to the edge of poverty are also driven to working long hours away from their families and their personal interests, driven to stress and anguish over the basic necessities of life and are too often driven to less than honorable means to escape the enslaving trap that binds them to the rat race. By hobbling people's options for creating prosperity and pleasant living conditions, you strangle their efforts to realize their goals in life. And this has the capacity to debilitate and demoralize people's—and hence a culture's—very character.

The second topic of each chapter will deal with: "The Solution." It outlines the policies of Social Viability—the roadmap out of our current predicament.

The seventh chapter will take the theory and information of the first six and boil it down into the very real and practical options you have before you. It will explain those actions which will most effectively contribute to the corruption and degeneration you see around you. And then it will juxtapose this with the measures you can take to generate the abundant prosperity, freedom, and security available with Social Viability.

If you have had enough of high-level corruption wreaking disaster and degradation, and you are ready to do something about it, then a magnificent future is yours to make for yourself, your family, your community, and your world. Read on and you will learn, in very real terms, the tangible actions that you can take to that end.

CHAPTER 1
PRIMARY CAUSE

THE PROBLEM: THE RULING PLUTOCRACY

Our Puppet Masters

IT SHOULD be clearly marked at the outset that the corruption, violence and disarray in the world today is a result of our own passive cooperation with the ruling global plutocracy. A plutocracy is a group that exercises power through wealth. It is a system whereby the super-wealthy rule. Despite what you have been led to believe, a plutocratic complex runs your society. Our rulers have good reason to tell you that you still live in a democracy or constitutional republic. However, it is far from true. They are simply shielding their activities and influence from public view.

Our society is not viable because its social structures and mechanisms have been designed by people who seek to exploit, enslave and imprison en masse. We are voluntary passengers on a craft piloted by crazy men and we are complicit in our own and our children's slow demise by way of our passive cooperation. We need to become familiar with the habits of these crazy plutocrats and withdraw our participation in their depraved designs for us.

Who are these crazy men? They are the small handful of families at the top of the food chain in international banking and finance. Through their myriad holdings, directorships and influences, they effectively own the world. What they don't literally own outright, owes them money or jumps at their orders. Over time they have erected economic contrivances and monetary systems that funnel wealth into their own hands, and through that wealth they control all other significant matters, political and social. We continue to use their money and so we perpetually elect them into power over our governments and our lives.

Democracy, constitutional republics and the separation of the powers of state were founded in an effort to combat the despotism of monarchs that used feudalism to organize, run and subjugate populations. Lords had money. They could buy soldiers. They dictated terms and laws to the serfs by way of force. The serfs obeyed, or else. This is correctly considered to be innately wrong. To exploit your fellow humans for your own benefit is the essential component of a criminal act.

Now, we face worse. The feudalistic tradition continues, but in this day and age the lords use their money to buy more than just soldiers. Now they also hire mass media organizations and governments that weave webs of deceit through the fabric of our society, leaving us in a mystery about the way our world really works. They know that they cannot enslave masses that know they are being exploited. These plutocratic lords have found, however, that if people can be led to believe their hard times are caused by cyclic recessions or vague market conditions, then they will turn their attention back to their favorite television sitcom or sporting event and remain obedient. If you confuse someone thoroughly enough concerning a particular subject by giving enough misleading and false information about it, the person will usually either ignore the subject altogether or they will memorize the lies and falsehoods, glibly reciting them whenever discussing the subject so as to give themselves the comforting impression that they grasp what is affecting their lives.

The truth is that these plutocrats dictate virtually everything of significance that happens in your society. They create the economic conditions of your society by regulating its money supply and fiscal policy. They direct your elected leaders by paying for their election campaigns and financing the lobbying groups that influence their legislation. They tell you what you can and can't do because those that make and enforce the laws are effectively in their employ. The industries that provide your necessities are owned outright or are in hock to these people. They even seek to take possession of your mind through the corporate media and the perverted education systems that they own and influence.

They run the society that you and your family depend upon. It is a small group of people. Their identities are somewhat hidden. And their motives are, at best, selfish. At worst, they are demonic. This is evident in their actions.

There are many corrupt and depraved influential people in plain view that are easy to condemn. But, it must be recognized, first and foremost, that the puppet masters pulling the strings from behind the scenes are at the crux of the issue. Any solution or reform to societal ills must take this matter into account or it will inevitably fail. Because network television doesn't cover the actions and dictates of these individuals, it can be easy to forget them or overlook their importance, but they are the tumor that is making society sick. All of the slimy, frantic and violent manifestations that you see on television news are but the symptoms.

Should we simply cut out this tumor? No, we should not. Many a cancer patient has had a malignant tumor surgically removed only to have more cancer emerge. If one fails to correct the habits that caused the malignancy to form, the problem persists. If the plutocratic criminals at the helm were somehow charged and brought to justice, the slime on the fringes of that sector of society would step right into their places if the fundamental economic and social infrastructure that allows them to exploit the population were not addressed thoroughly.

Many other cancer victims have saved themselves by reassessing how they care for their bodies and their minds, and have formed new habits that cure the illness. These people tend to remain cured for life. Having addressed the fundamental causes generating the disease, the cancer goes into remission and is eventually cured altogether.

The answer is to reform those habits that have caused this social tumor to grow in the first place—to rehabilitate by establishing new methods of caring for our society, its people and its systems of interchange.

And this is precisely what Social Viability deals with.

Machiavellianism

It is quite crucial to clearly understand the Machiavellian way in which the ruling plutocrats manipulate our world's affairs. You must grasp this modus operandi in order to both eliminate their control over how you react to events in the world around you and to allow you to recognize the value in social systems that counteract these techniques.

It is common for these puppet masters to create an urgent problem that will induce a fearful reaction and then to introduce solutions that apparently address the urgent problem but which are actually designed to serve their own unannounced agenda. Stated differently: manufacture a problem so as to elicit an emotional reaction that paves the way for a solution that covertly enslaves those desperate for the solution. This is a vital principle to grasp in recognizing Machiavellian maneuvers because in order to divide and conquer, it is necessary to create artificial enemies. The easiest way to create enemies is to generate violent problems that can be blamed on one party or another.

The resources of the puppet masters are vast. They have the means to create all manner of disasters through front groups, faithful organizations and subservient government agencies. You may ask, "How on Earth can anyone discern the influences at work behind tumultuous events?" It is a valid question because it is often impossible to know, firsthand, exactly what is happening behind the scenes. But if one can read into events effectively, one can know enough about an event to know how to react and how not to react. And it is quite a simple thing to do.

The key component to recognize is: MOTIVE. This cannot be stressed enough. Detectives must weigh motive into homicide investigations and so should you. Motive needs to be one of the first elements you consider when observing events that negatively influence society. One must discipline oneself to ignore the noise and emotional hype ignited in the news media by violent and disturbing events, and to look first and foremost at the motive behind the event.

Who stands to gain the most from the event? Of these people/groups who has the capacity, connections and influence to orchestrate or perpetrate such an event? With this list, one can then watch successive events and actions unfold with a viewpoint that will allow one to see clearly who most likely influenced, orchestrated and/or directly perpetrated the event. This analysis applies to any event that is destructive to social functioning and human life and that is carried out by the hand of men. Terrorist attacks, military invasions and assassinations are glaring examples, but one must not totally ignore seemingly random or natural phenomena.

It is vital to look beyond the reality presented to one by propaganda organizations and view market calamities, famine, disease, apparent accidents and even natural disasters critically. Economic problems can be created at the drop of a hat by those that control the money supply. Markets can be crashed and dire food shortages can easily be brought about by the financially powerful. Deadly diseases can be set loose. Aircraft and automobiles can be sabotaged. And modern technology certainly exists to manipulate weather and seismic conditions. No, not all disasters and accidents come directly at the hands of evil men, but one must never rule anything out as far-fetched or paranoid before examining the facts in any given case, especially when suspicious actions from shifty people come in response to the event.

One of the things that separate humans from the rest of the animal kingdom is our ability to analyze facts. If one dismisses possibilities before looking at the facts because of preconceived notions, the facts are never viewed, analysis is never conducted, and that which makes us human is not exercised. Be an alert, thinking, analytical human being; not a beast in a herd.

Getting back to the issue of motive, be alert to people and organizations that assign blame quickly in the wake of violent events, especially when these accusations are made of those that have little or no reasonable motive, or where the purported motive is unlikely or specious. One can sometimes quickly locate a suspect by listening to them toss allegations and accusations. A casual investigation of such individuals will sometimes reveal strong and compelling motives of their own.

One historical example of these Machiavellian techniques is the burning of the Reichstag by the Nazis. It created the problem of so-called communist attacks on their nation. The reaction of the people allowed Hitler to present the solution of being granted dictatorial powers to help fight that supposed threat. Hitler's political party had great motive for the attack in using it as a pretext to seize greater control. The nebulous "communists" had very little or no tactical motive in burning a parliamentary building.

Another example is Israel's Mossad reportedly having a hand in the founding of Hamas back in the early 1970's. It can be claimed that this was merely a covert effort to combat the PLO, and this may well be the case on the surface. However, that this has directly led to sustained, heinous violence against Israel which, in turn, has been used to justify the solution of military action against Palestinians time and again cannot be ignored. Those in the business of arms manufacturing, for instance, have profited enormously from this continued violence.

One more example is elements within the United States federal government being involved in the events of September 11, 2001. Everyone living though that event is familiar with the reaction of the public in the U.S. These horrified and enraged reactions paved the way for the federal government's solution which was to push through Draconian laws under the USA PATRIOT Act and to quickly launch two foreign invasions. It must be noted that U.S. President Bush blamed a specific group of Islamic terrorists for the attack almost immediately. The corporate media threw Osama Bin Laden's name out well before any investigation could have yielded any useful results. Is there any solid motive there for Islamic terrorists to commit such an act? Is a group that has the capability to pull off such an attack and that supposedly wants to defeat America really going to attack office buildings?

On the other hand, President Bush's family (along with many others that have holdings in the arms industry) has profited financially from the ensuing wars. Another major beneficiary has been the owners and advertisers in the mass media. Viewer ratings would never have been higher in history than in the days and weeks following those events in 2001.

Essential in the execution of any such Machiavellian stunt is the creation of an enemy for the masses to hate. A problem by its very nature requires some opposing force.

Divide and conquer. Give the people an enemy. Commit atrocities against the people and blame it on an enemy. Give the people a solution that enslaves them. As elementary as it is, most seem to be ignorant of the maneuver when it used on them.

This modus operandi of these covert rulers of ours is important to keep in mind when unraveling the web of deceit that has been wound around the public's eyes. Don't be fooled. Furthermore, learn to recognize social organizations whose policies make Machiavellian ploys difficult or impossible to use. These are the types of institutions that we will use to climb out of the mess that we, the human race, have let ourselves be led into.

Communism & Capitalism

A pet myth that our ruling plutocrats have used in creating enemies is that concerning the economic formats of capitalism and socialism. The basic myth is that they are opposite or even very different systems. They are simply variations of the same operating basis revolving around the concept of a monopoly.

Neither format is effective, both are poorly understood— like the very subject of economics itself—and the whole contention concerning these supposedly opposing schools of thought is largely the product of a more basic lack in the methodology of the subject. These convoluted methods for managing economies exist simply because there are no useful means for measuring economic activity. Currencies are supposed to be used to measure economic activity but the currencies themselves have floating, arbitrary values. It is like an engineer taking measurements of "about this much." Men are prone to getting very tangled up devising complicated, ineffective mechanisms to compensate for basic inadequacies in a system and there is no more glaring example of this than in the subject of economics.

In the case of capitalism, the whole driving force of the economic system is the self-interested attempt to ultimately secure and maintain a monopoly. With a capitalist system, the open market and its laws of supply and demand, coupled with the self-interest of the businesses and individuals involved, apply an "invisible hand" to the economic factors managing production and distribution. I have no argument with the existence of this observable phenomenon. A business may supply an area where a product is needed so as to make a profit. That often does result in a product being offered in an area where it is needed or desired. And yes, competition between businesses in an industry will cause the prices to be driven down and efficiency driven up so as to be competitive.

What I do have a problem with is the utter lack of a valid economic playing field on which to compete. The money—that which is supposed to be a measurement of value—is elastic. Businesses are forced, by necessity of competition, to use childish sales tricks, covert marketing ploys and general haggling maneuvers to remain competitive. These tactics are most often nothing more than manipulations of value so as to gain some advantage in a treacherous economic environment. These are the tools of the trade of any successful merchant and it is a direct result of the undefined value of currency.

A builder does not manipulate the length of an inch depending on how much timber he has on hand. But this is exactly what a merchant does when he uses supply and demand to set the price of his wares.

When businesses must spend more time on negotiating deals, price shopping and haggling than on improving the quality and efficiency of their production processes, you end up with an environment of people scrambling, fighting tooth and nail, trying to rip one another off in an effort to make a profit and secure a greater market share—which has, of course, the ultimate aim of securing a monopoly on the market. To survive in such a system necessitates stinging your customers for as much as you can get away with so as to make a decent profit. If you don't screw your costs down as tightly as possible on your expenses side and screw your customers for as much money as you can get out of them on the sales side, you get screwed by your competition who are, themselves, screwing the screws as tightly as they can. Everyone screws everyone else (including members of the same team in disputes between employees and employers over what is fair pay) for whatever they can get away with as they learn to just live with their consciences. The system breeds criminality and the biggest cheats too often wind up at the top of the financial pile. All the while good workers get laid off to cut costs and product quality is sacrificed, all in the name of profit margins. Yes, theoretically in capitalism you will never see an absolute sustained monopoly, but must we have all the economic carnage in the form of lost fortunes, failed businesses and lay-offs along the way?

Furthermore, central to the doctrine of capitalism is the practice of bankers leveraging capital (including the pretend capital employed in the fractional reserve brand of banking) by charging interest on loans. Having an entire sector of society make obscene amounts of money out of merely having capital is ludicrous. There is no productive basis—no benefit to society—in such a practice. That wealth absorbed comes from somewhere: the rest of productive society. Allowing bankers to leverage their capital so as to leech off the working class puts a very ugly face on capitalism, no doubt.

As it stands, despite its theoretical axioms, the "capitalist" system so beloved in the West is so monopolized that it is, for many practical purposes, more like a dictatorial communism. In the most vital sectors of society we see apparent competition that is merely a farce hiding a small cabal of puppet masters owning multiple "competing" interests.

And that is exactly where our "capitalist" banker-masters want us to be. They have secured their monopolies and any capitalist who can secure and maintain a monopoly is in heaven. A monopoly that covers all industry and all sectors is the ultimate socialism. Extend that to a giant governmental monopoly and you have that horrible enemy, communism, all neatly secured and maintained using the force of a monstrous Orwellian super-government, in charge of one and all, deciding who works where and who gets what—and all right here in our own "capitalist" backyard.

As for communism, the slogan sounds very humanitarian: "From each according to his ability, to each according to his need." However, in practice it fails miserably. Why? Most importantly, the position at the head of a socialist/communist government, with all of the power that would bestow such a person, is the sort of position that would attract individuals of malicious intent like filth attracts flies. People who habitually bring harm to others are in continual fear of persecution for their criminal acts. Hence, the most attractive position for such an individual is in a position of high rank where he is above the law by way of being an enforcer of the law. Even if the theoretical methodologies of socialism and communism were sound (which they are not), the corruption that gathers in such positions would wreak havoc. No system or methodology is immune to corruption.

Furthermore, the people under such subjection are a far cry from free. Without real choice of endeavor in life, you become a human-robot hybrid.

Additionally, with the most productive being the most heavily taxed, incentive to work hard goes out the window and decent productivity follows closely behind.

The inevitable ne plus ultra of socialism, the ultimate fulfillment of communism, is that infamous Orwellian dictatorship. Capitalism is too often a euphemism for profiteering and leads right down the road to fascism time and again. And it is a fine shade of grey indeed between fascism and communism when you boil it down to the end results for Joe and Jane Smith living on Average Street. To pretend that there are two sides in the equation only serves to make enemies out of people and rob both sides blind in the process.

It is a farce and the world at large is falling for it to the degree that no one even mentions economic systems other than those whose successes are determined by their relative monopolization of markets. It is like two men arguing about who has the faster carrier pigeon while ignoring a ringing telephone.

Their Downfall

The primary downfall of these concealed rulers of ours is that they are maniacs. Maniacs do crazy things and tend to foul themselves up, no matter how intelligent or powerful they are. Testament to this is how slow and tedious their progress toward their goal has been. If they were truly efficient in their efforts, we would have long since been living in the full realization of the Orwellian global-state. They hold all the aces; they have all the resources needed at their disposal. George Orwell seemed to be estimating that the despotic global tyranny spelled out in his famous book would be realized by that year: 1984. He was making an educated assessment from the standpoint of a reasonable and productive individual. And our plutocrats should have achieved their ultimate goals by that time. The problem for them is that they sabotage themselves by betraying their basic humanity. Any man lost in a confused attempt to commit evil will continually trip over his own innate sense of right and wrong. It is inevitable.

Most importantly, they are outnumbered, and this is the joker they will never hold in their hand. The vast majority of the population consists of good people trying to make their way and live up to decent values. They may get confused, desperate or misled, but they are nevertheless trying to do the right thing. Just by that simple fact, the masses are working against the puppet masters' agenda. People don't wish to be enslaved or live in a degraded society. They work against it naturally. They must be tricked and fooled every step of the way, and doing so weaves very intricate and fragile webs of lies and deceit that the agents of our leaders inevitably find difficult and cumbersome to work with when doing their masters' bidding. This is why when one takes the time to pull the curtain back and look behind the "official story" one sees almost comical blundering, botched operations, and ridiculous charades.

Furthermore, they derive their power from us. Their power consists solely of the authority we grant them. If, collectively, we cease to participate in their game, they lose their power. They depend on us. We, however, do not depend on them. We have been fooled into granting them their power. Once that flimsy veil is lifted, it will require but a simple collective decision to dethrone our covert rulers.

Finally, they are terribly frightened. They fear, more than anything, the prospect of their atrocities coming to light.

They fear that if their crimes were made public, they would be treated in the cruel and barbaric manner they treat their victims. That fear breeds extreme tentativeness and neurotic caution. This cannot help but slow their progress. They lack the truly proud confidence and unchecked conviction that allows a righteous man to bring about swift change and great improvement.

These things are all in our favor. We must take advantage of the time given us, for while our advantage is that their incompetence has given us time to effect change, our disadvantage is the inevitability of suffering if we fail to act successfully.

Additionally, it must be considered that in their frantic and conflicted efforts, they may drop the bundle altogether. Their mechanisms of influence are prone to catastrophic failure, even by their own standards. Our social systems, having been built upon ulterior motives and blatantly foolish premises, are prone to breakdown. We cannot trust those in power to hold our society and its economic systems together for us. If they don't deliberately pull the rug out from under us, they will sooner or later fail through criminal incompetence and leave us high and dry.

THE SOLUTION: SOCIAL VIABILITY

Function & Product

The function of Social Viability is to act as a point of agreement between productive people. It is a membership organization that uses statements of policy, such as this text, as a basis for social organization and coordination. It issues no law and enforces no allegiance. It does reserve the right to revoke membership, just as each member reserves the right to withdraw their support and participation.

Its policy provides a framework for individuals and enterprises to interact and so turn the wheels of modern society. In doing so, this function must remain riveted to and guided by one very simple but important idea: Eschew decay and build prosperity.

On the surface this could be taken as simply to avoid the morally corrupt and the criminally inclined, and to do your best to be productive and lead a healthy life. While this is encompassed and embraced by the idea, in the context of Social Viability it means a great deal more.

There are definite and practical actions you can take to defeat the efforts of the plutocrats to enslave you. It revolves around one simple activity over which you can exert direct and measurable control. I will explain exactly what that is here.

The plutocratic puppet masters and virtually all of their oppressive means depend upon their control of the money we use. Money is the lifeblood of a society and culture. It is the practical, everyday thing that directly links everyone in a nation. It is the medium upon which all growth and prosperity—or decay and deprivation—rides. You are controlled and dictated to because your money—how much is circulating in your economy, how much of it you can earn, how most of it is spent and through what hands it passes—is all controlled. Banks, governments, and other plutocrat-controlled institutions wield far too great an influence in defining the financial boundaries of your life due to their control of your money.

The plutocrats will lose their grip on society and culture when we stop using their money. If we do not use their money, their banks will go out of business and their governments will shut down as their tax revenue vanishes.

This is crucial. This forms the core of our strategy: When we stop using their money, their power will vanish. The hope of mankind in throwing off the yoke of the present plutocratic rule is contained in this concept. All we need to do is stop using the money that they supply us and start using an alternative currency.

This point cannot be understated. A plutocrat—by his very nature—rules by way of money. That is the key to dethroning them and liberating our culture.

We must stop using their money. However, money is necessary in technologically developed societies. To simply stop using money in some form or another is entirely impractical and would be utterly disastrous.

Social Viability uses a new and much more effective breed of money. It has entirely unique policies regarding currency and commercial trading. The nature of these policies guard against the corruption that has befallen our current means of economic exchange and allows you to engage in wealth building in an ethical, worthwhile and effective manner, free from the encumbrance of today's economic burdens.

The transition to a new currency that functions according to the principles of Social Viability is limited only by the number of other people, producers, and service providers that use that same currency. As you find more people willing to take action to nullify the ruling plutocracy, you will be more able to use alternative currency and render the puppet masters' banks and governments impotent.

Social Viability must then employ social management organizations to supplant the failed management of social infrastructure. Social management will need to be continued when governments fail and cultural cohesion will need to be maintained as the corrupted establishments fall into disarray as their corrupted currencies fail.

In abstaining from the use of the established monetary system, you are eschewing decay; you are disconnecting from the control mechanism that wields command over your life and advances the decay of our society and culture. Engaging in trade according to the tenets of Social Viability, you are promoting and building prosperity, you are advocating stable economic development, and you are helping to erect a new social and cultural paradigm that may grow from out of the decay.

Again, the basic function of Social Viability is to provide policy that facilitates people's efforts to eschew decay and build prosperity. And the primary end product that results is: Time.

This is important: The essential end product of Social Viability is time. Time for you to build a life. Time for you to pursue interests and purposes which give you inspiration. Time for you to invent new technology. Time for you to spend with your family and nurture your children's development. Time for you to reach for higher states, personally and spiritually.

And when considering time, one must consider money. Time is nothing more than a relative measurement of how much we are getting done. What is money? A practical measurement of how much we are getting done. Theoretically, if you do a lot of work, you earn a lot of money. Then you can take some time off work because you have saved enough money to support yourself for a time without further income.

Benjamin Franklin had it right. Time is money. Literally. No more, no less. Money in the bank is time accrued to use to your desire. If you save $20,000 by giving up your time at your profession, serving others, you can then take that money and buy an automobile, which essentially means that you are converting that $20,000 into the time it took other people to construct that automobile. The makers of the automobile then, in turn, spend their share of the money collected by converting it into other producers' and service providers' time to acquire other desirables. And so the cogs of an economy turn; the central element being time, the currency merely the exchangeable representation of people's time.

So when we consider that the product of Social Viability is time, we must understand that this includes saved time and monetary wealth. Social Viability exists to give you a life which is not ruled by an occupation or a rat race. It exists to allow you to rapidly generate wealth as saved time, whatever you do, however you choose to be of service to others. Social Viability's economic methodology allows this for every profession and occupation. You do not and should not have to be a banking swindler, opportunistic lawyer, gifted salesperson, high-strung executive, genius entrepreneur, talented entertainer or lottery winner to achieve this—just an honest, willing, productive person. It is not only possible, it is entirely practical and is as it should be.

Goals & Purposes

The ultimate goal of the systems of Social Viability is: To have the culture and community of people on Earth living and working viably without undue oppression; actively, effectively, perpetually building and developing better conditions for mankind.

The following secondary purposes are requisite to and implicit in that ultimate goal:

1. Bring together like-minded people interested in building a new society out of the commotion that exists here at the beginning of the 21st century.

2. Dissolve the influence of the ruling plutocracy by ceasing to participate in their corrupted and dysfunctional society. If we cease to use their banks and take part in their economy, then they will lose us and the money that is extorted and taxed out of us. Their leverage over us will evaporate.

3. As the infrastructure of the current society comes undone, replace it with viable and functioning industries and institutions that are well-organized and cooperating according to sound principles.

4. Restore neglected, valid institutions and technologies, and foster the development of new technologies and means that have been stultified by perverted interests.

The details on each of these purposes will be spelled out later and you will see how relatively simple it is to accomplish. Yes, actions such as this may be met with violent resistance from the interests and agents of the plutocrats in power. However, our alternatives are naught and the rewards of seeing it through are potentially phenomenal. How ugly it gets depends entirely upon how rapidly and effectively we execute our strategy.

That strategy must revolve around an economic objective. We must implement new systems of exchange using a brand new currency and rapidly put it into use across a broad spectrum of societal function. If people, families, companies, industries and entire societies can implement a new currency and function effectively, they will at once free themselves from the influence of the plutocracy's banking system that currently owns them.

Decentralization of Social Administration

In the establishment of a new and viable society, we must keep in mind the errors of old and the systems which played into the hands of the conspirators that seek to make slaves of men. One of the primary factors contributing to our current predicament is the monopolization of government. The apparent controlling and issuing of legal tender, the administration of public interests and all legal functions are held by a monopoly in any given geographical location. Government is that monopoly. Any other industrial monopolies are rightly rejected as being potentially detrimental to society at large. Yet government maintains this accepted monopoly. People seem to take it for granted and regard it as necessary or simply logical.

It is, however, neither logical nor necessary. It is so because it is convenient for the plutocrats since they merely have to buy up and corrupt the politicians in one government to gain control of any given country and all of the people that happen to live in that country. The people are left with few choices.

Imagine an auto mechanic that was granted a monopoly like that which government enjoys. He could enforce regulations that dictated when your car needed maintenance or repair. He could fix your car in the manner he prescribed and could charge you the amount he saw fit, extracting it from your paycheck before you even saw the money. If he then decided that he would like more power and money he could do one or both of two things. He could raise the cost of maintenance and repair or he could hire criminals to vandalize and sabotage your car so as to incur more needs for repair. And we find that this is the manner in which our governments too often behave.

The plutocrats would not be able to exert such convenient control over society if government were not monopolized. Even in a democracy, once the candidates of each of the major political parties are purchased by the plutocrats, the election becomes a mere public show, as significant as a football game, less exciting than a game of cards—unless of course you are under the spell of the media and believe that there is any validity left in the democratic process in any major power on Earth. Once the plutocratic puppet masters have purchased their government monopoly—their puppets—they may do as they wish.

What is needed is decentralization of the government— or more correctly—of the social management.

And it is important to treat the subject as social management rather than government. To *govern* implies, if not clearly denotes, a ruling of subordinate masses. This is an invalid notion since all strata of society are equally necessary to its operation and therefore of equal importance. Social management simply denotes attending to the administrative functions that allow a society to function smoothly. It primarily deals with coordinating economic and infrastructural functions and should never deal with telling the public how they should behave. This is crucial. When a society begins down the path of having its government behave more like a custodian than a service provider, it has set its course for cultural dissolution and tyranny.

The social management needs to be de-monopolized. A citizen is as free as he has choices and if a citizen is disgusted with the service provided by the government for which he pays, he should have every right to withdraw his support and seek services elsewhere. Your auto mechanic must provide a good service at a reasonable price or you will take your car elsewhere to be repaired and maintained.

Why should government be immune to such naturally corrective conditions? The answer: It is not in the interests of the plutocratic puppet masters that are calling the shots. If people have the option of forming and using separate social management enterprises, the establishment is kept honest. If any of the individual management enterprises begin to engage in corrupt dealings, people can simply walk away and discontinue the use of their services without having to emigrate from the country.

To be clear, Social Viability is not a social management organization. It is a membership organization that simply announces philosophies, principles and policies that people can agree to and can use to organize a society with. Allowing competition in social management is one of those principles by which Social Viability operates. The administrators of Social Viability membership organizations can contract or charter social management enterprises to attend to the various public functions as needed. If the leaders of a Social Viability organization contracted or retained inept or corrupt social managers, they would lose members. Simple.

Social Organization

Industry within any given society needs to be arranged so that independent interests do not conflict with or counteract one another. If all industries and sectors have their purposes aligned in a cooperative manner, society is able to function in an efficient and effective manner. Just as a person's sanity could be gauged by the amount of conflicted emotion he experiences and the number of conflicting ideas he expresses, a society's relative sanity can be gauged by the number of conflicting interests and influences it has among its constituent individuals, groups, organizations, industries and sectors.

Crucial to accomplishing social sanity is correct adoption of production objectives.

The society must be correctly oriented around beneficial production objectives, as must each division and department of a society. Each organization and enterprise must have its own clearly defined production objective that contributes to and supports the production objective of the social department in which it resides.

In today's society, entire industries operate according to perverted production objectives that counteract the well-being of the society in general, and this alone carries the potential to destroy a civilization if left unchecked.

As an illustration of the kind of mess that can occur through errant adoption of production objectives, let's take a look at one glaring example: the multi-billion-dollar pharmaceutical industry. The production objective that the corporations in this sector have adopted is <u>patented drugs sold</u>. This is dangerous because a requisite condition for the sale of these drugs is sick and unhealthy people. If everyone were healthy and happy, the entire industry's business would utterly dry up. An industry as lucrative as the pharmaceutical industry is never going to allow their business to dry up. They are going to do everything in their formidable power to make sure there are enough sick and unhealthy people around to ensure their business continues and even improves.

If they genuinely adopted the production objective of healthy people, they would cease selling the vast majority of the medications they put on the market. These drugs merely alleviate symptoms. They not only fail to address the root illness, they can exacerbate the illness itself and will also create new conditions that require other drugs. For example, there is no greater travesty of common sense in modern society than the systematic drugging with psychiatric medication of upset or depressed people. These kinds of widespread lunacies are perpetrated as a direct result of invalid and destructive production objectives being widely tolerated and even endorsed in modern society.

Another salient example is the arms manufacturing industry. Their production objective is munitions sold. For weapons and ammunition to be sold in a steady supply, they need to be used. For weapons and ammunition to be used, wars need to be incited. Anyone still wonder why our governments wage ineptly planned and poorly justified warfare? The immeasurable volume of slaughter and tumult perpetrated in the wars of history can be attributed to the invalid adoption of, and ignorance concerning, correct production objectives. If the production objective of munitions sold is changed to safe and secure nations, all this carnage can cease. True, the plutocratic criminals will lose a very profitable mechanism with which to siphon off wealth from the populace, but the rest of civilization will have the opportunity to enjoy sustained peace. Reasonable trade-off, yes?

More of these perverted industries will be dealt with in more detail in a later chapter. For now, the point must be restated so as to be as clear as possible: production objectives must be adopted and must align with the greater good of the society at large. Production objectives must be assigned to every division, department, industry, organization, post and position in society. The wider the scope of an activity, the more crucial the production objective; the most crucial production objective would be that of the entire society.

Each society must be structured around—must have as its production objective—the production of exportable goods and services that are beneficial to the consumers of the products and services.

Today, societies are structured around geographical boundaries. Much of the social focus is on the governments that lay claim to geographical boundaries and the power they wield. The production objective of contemporary government is geopolitical power. For the vast majority of fools currently in public office, economic wealth is not a means unto providing better quality of living for their nations' citizens but rather a weapon to use in gaining their production objective: <u>geopolitical power</u>.   Hence   the   shortsighted,   deceptive,   arrogant, degenerative manner in which most modern governments behave.

Societies and their production will naturally be influenced by geography. But the notion of social boundaries being defined by geography is outdated. The social boundaries need to be defined by productivity and must be built around the production of exportable goods and services. When the ultimate production objectives and hence, the focus of societies are the exported goods and services, wealth will be generated, high quality of living will come easily and naturally, and the citizens will have more time/money to live their lives according to their own unique inspiration.

<u>Membership & Citizenry</u>

There are no qualifications required for membership with Social Viability other than not being a known antagonist of Social Viability or an associate of such a person. Parents and guardians may register children in their care if they, themselves, are members.

There are no special privileges afforded a member. A member that meets certain qualifications with respect to productivity, knowledge and benevolence may be ranked as a citizen. A citizen may be afforded certain privileges.

Under the policy of Social Viability, pricing is not used to restrict demand of items on the market that are in limited supply. Alternatively, ranking may be used to decide to whom such nonessential goods are sold if the demand is greater than the supply. Eligibility for social management offices should certainly be dependent upon the relative citizen ranking of an applicant for such a position. Also, citizens are given priority in the granting of financial loans according to their rank.

Those that contribute to the growth of society through significant personal production, through familial production, through entrepreneurial activity and through social service should be rewarded with preferential treatment. People's social rights must be earned in Social Viability. Rights and restrictions are at opposite ends of the same spectrum that must be applied in relation to how valuable a person has shown themselves to be to their fellows. To do otherwise provides little social incentive to be a productive citizen, and then everyone suffers. A criminal must not have the same rights as a benevolent leader of men or an inventor of technology. Rights give one freedom to influence those around one. People should be given rights in proportion to their demonstrated benevolence and competence. Those who belligerently demand rights without having done anything to earn them are asking for the privilege to influence others irrespective of any malevolence or incompetence.

CHAPTER 2
LEGITIMATE TRADE

THE PROBLEM: BANKING & FINANCE

Loans & Interest

O NE of the more salient departures from intelligent reasoning that we, the general populace, have tolerated is the charging of interest on loans extended by banks and financial institutions. It is common and accepted, but it is essentially a criminal activity and a tremendous burden upon the economies of the world.

It is true that loans should be extended to those who need it or to those that aim to generate productivity with that temporary extension of funds. But it is the height of folly to allow the wealthy sector of society to make massive fortunes from interest imposed on the rest of the population in the process. This is one of the primary means of economic suppression of productive people by the bankers and financiers. It is their free ride—and a luxurious ride it is.

When a modern bank lends money to a person it is, in reality, extending credit on behalf of the entire society and its economy. In this day and age, they do not lend reserves. The money is created out of thin air; electronically entered into the system. That money loaned is spent on goods and services throughout the community. Those that sell the person the goods with the borrowed money are really the ones extending the credit in real terms concerning real commodities. Consumption without prior contribution is what occurs when someone spends the money from a loan that hasn't yet been repaid. Consumption without prior contribution places a burden upon the economy—the economy which everyone in a society supports. When a bank makes a loan, it is making it on behalf of everyone in the society, yet the interest payments are claimed as private profit.

At one point in time, the fact that banks were lending money they had in actual reserves—that had been earned by honestly productive account holders—served as a guarantee that their loans would not overextend the resources of the economy. However, the value of the dollar (or any other floating value currency for that matter) has been so far lost into the abyss of the manipulated markets, it has ceased to have any meaningful, tangible value that can be honestly connected to the actual goods and services the dollar is supposed to represent.

Furthermore, the fractional reserve banking method has left any sense of sound reasoning on this subject far behind. The principles of the system defy logic to the point of being comical. Banks not only generate for themselves an obscene return on money that belongs to others (the account holders), but they also lend money that doesn't even exist up to an arbitrarily chosen multiple of their reserves. The bankers are, in fact, granting the right to debtors to obtain goods and services from producers and service providers on credit, and then having those debtors repay the advantage gained by the loan (known commonly as "interest") back to the bankers themselves in return for the favor, rather than to the producers and service providers that actually extended the tangible commodities and labor to the debtor. Productive society was the entity that did the debtor the favor of loaning them goods and services. The banks simply hold the money which is a mechanism of trade. They don't own the money (except by illegitimate means) and so deserve no repayment of interest.

Money is a trade tool that represents goods and services. It allows people to trade freely without having to resort to direct barter. Modern currencies are not commodities and should not be treated as such. When fiat currencies are treated like commodities, prosperity and wealth get sucked away from the functioning economy and funneled into the hands of the idle who exploit it. To make money by trading money as though it were a real commodity is a corruption of the tool of money. It places a burden on everyone else in the economy and causes idle and useless sectors to become very affluent.

When sectors that generate no real benefit to society are allowed to siphon away large volumes of wealth, you allow a monster to grow. You get what you reward and when you reward corruption with wealth, you wind up with wealthy corrupt individuals collectively sucking upon the vitality of the society like a tenacious and insatiable giant leech.

Investors that inject capital into the economy should be rewarded, but their reward should not come by way of sucking the financial life out families and businesses through usurious interest as is practiced by the banking sector. And the lending should not be done with such avarice as to jeopardize an entire society's economy.

Just conceive of the raw volume of money collected by banks and financial institutions in loan, mortgage and credit card interest alone, and you are looking at the potential immediate return of wealth to the society's economy—to yours and my pockets—just by replacing this industry with organizations that apply sensible policies concerning money and lending. This barely scrapes the surface of the economic erosion these institutions perpetrate but is, alone, significant enough to consider as a major threat to the viability and integrity of our societies.

Central Banking

No discourse on the banking and finance industry would be complete without at least a brief look at one of the most blatantly crooked institutions on Earth: the Federal Reserve System in the United States. If it is possible to outdo the ridiculous charade that is the fractional reserve lending arrangement banks use, this is it. It is possibly one of the most ludicrous ideas ever devised and seems to have been specifically designed to bring a nation to its knees financially. The only thing more insane than the system itself is the lack of public outcry concerning its methods of operation.

The tragic results of our forebears' and our own failure to abolish this arrangement are deep and devastating.

The Federal Reserve is essentially lending the money printed by the government back to the government and the citizens as if it had a legitimate claim to that money. If you were to print money in your basement and then spend it, you would be thrown in prison for counterfeiting. Yet that is essentially what the Federal Reserve—a private consortium of banks, not a government institution—is doing.

They are making a massive illegitimate profit at your expense. The money they print and use as their own reduces the value and buying power of the money you have earned. They are, in effect, stealing money right out of your pocket on an ongoing basis. It is the biggest criminal scam in modern history.

These central bankers are the driving force behind the formation of the European Union and the planned merging of nations on the American continents. The larger the population using a single currency, the more money they can make— literally. The more people, the greater the capacity to absorb the inflationary impact of their counterfeiting program, the more money they can print for themselves.

Furthermore the Federal Reserve is artificially propping up an insolvent economy in the United States. If a family continued to borrow and borrow, racking up debts with credit cards, loans and mortgages, spending more money than they were earning, they would seem to be very affluent at first glance, living in mansions and driving luxury cars, but they would be headed for eventual financial ruin. Such a family would live as depraved professional consumers.

We're all familiar with the concept of a spoiled brat. The youngster who has been given the world and worked for nothing becomes a lazy, demanding, pouting degenerate. They come to expect that they be given everything without contributing anything. Tabloid magazines love to obsess over the worst examples of this phenomenon in celebrity circles, and hardworking folk can't help but shake their heads at them.

A person is not happy when they have not worked for and fairly earned those things they have. And neither is a nation. Just like the wealthy parent that gives expensive gifts to their child, the Federal Reserve, by pumping up the United States economy with inflation, is creating a spoiled brat populace. More and more Americans are becoming lazy, demanding, pouting degenerates. What was once very rare is becoming more and more commonplace. It is one of the greatest cultural tragedies in history: The United States was born in a hardworking, courageous, down-to-earth tradition and through these values its people built a superpower.

Now, with all of the money being printed and with all of the borrowing of the federal government, the United States has become that family that has run up its credit cards to their limit and that, despite its apparent wealth, is destined for financial ruin.

With the abundance of money in circulation, symptoms such as illegal immigration are inevitable. There is just more money in the United States. The fact that it is borrowed and printed out of thin air makes it an artificial wealth, but that makes no immediate difference to working folk who are happy to have plenty of money in their pockets.

However, it does breed that spoiled brat mentality that is so far removed from the values that built America. The culture and economy of the United States has been, and is further being, subverted and dismantled and generally fed to the dogs. Productivity is being abandoned for consumerism; enterprise for opportunism.

Outsourcing of manufacturing and the carefully crafted marketing that is fed through the news and entertainment media is further exacerbating the problem that is illustrated when people's lives revolve around shopping malls and car dealerships rather than productive entrepreneurial ambition. The focus of people's lives being the consumption of goods and services is indicative of the United States economy consuming more than it is producing. Any economy that consumes at a rate greater than that at which it produces is doomed, just like the household that spends more than it makes.

Debt is slowly killing the United States and, with it, the industrialized world. And it is the Federal Reserve invoking that debt with the help of their corrupt politicians. The policies and practices of the Federal Reserve are cultivating a condition that has already wreaked cultural degeneration and which will inevitably end in economic disaster.

Remove the burden of the Federal Reserve System and its central banking counterparts around the world and a great prosperity will be restored to the productive people of the world.

Inflation

Another seemingly tragic failure in logic that is an intrinsic part of our economic systems is the floating value of the dollar. I use the word *seemingly* because there is very sound logic behind the system if your goal is to manipulate and exploit unsuspecting serfs. There is an absence in logic when one looks at the subject from the standpoint of trying to promote stable, effective, prosperous social and economic conditions.

Again, the dollar—any currency—represents the goods and services that we produce, trade and consume. It measures the relative value of the things we trade in our society. To remove it from a definite and tangible value that can be solidly connected to commodities being traded and leave it to the fickle vagaries of traders influenced by all manner of Wall Street propaganda is laughable. But that is what we face. Even the gold standard for the dollar was far from ideal, but at least it was something. To let a market determine the relative value of the dollar is as idiotic as letting a market determine how far it is from London to New York. Your time spent earning a living is too valuable to leave it to some greedy suits on Wall Street to dictate its worth to you.

This idiotic practice of floating currency values can be seen as nothing more than another artifice to loot wealth from the economy and from your wallet.

When money is printed and the central banks introduce it into the economy, the value of the dollar decreases and the price of goods and services begin to rise. The first to raise their prices to match the adjusted value of the currency are the ones that benefit. At the wealthier end of the economic spectrum, where cash flow is abundant and price increases are easily tolerated, prices, fees and taxes raise quickly to meet inflation. This filters on down through the rest of the economy to the regular consumer goods that you and I pay for. It happens faster in more active marketplaces—usually in big cities—than it does in less economically fervent areas. This is why goods and services cost more in Manhattan than they do in a small rural town. It is simple opportunism. Businesses in Manhattan can jack up their prices and still find a lot of customers and clients with the money to pay. In a small town there is less money moving around and far fewer people willing to expend more money than they really have to. It takes more time for the effects of inflation to filter down to less populated and less wealthy areas.

One of the last things to increase in response to inflation is the pay of wage earners. Hourly wages for most, in fact, never catch up to the actual value of the dollar and struggle to keep pace with the increasing prices of regular consumer goods. In effect, if you are a wage earner, the money you earn drops in value as soon as you are paid. The difference between the value of the dollar you earn and the value of the dollar you spend is greater the lower you are on the income scale. The rich get richer and the poor get poorer, and too often only because the rich make the rules.

Wall Street Trading

And now we come to the gambling rackets that are the stock, commodity, derivative and currency markets. To artificially inflate these markets and push their collective values higher and higher does nothing except drive money into the hands of the criminally inclined and the morally corrupt. Intrinsic value has become so obscured and so detached from reality that it is, at best, childish and, at worst, a social disaster waiting to happen.

Many of these markets began with valid and useful purposes. Pooling capital through stocks is a valid practice. The trade of commodities is utterly necessary to a modern economy. Many derivative contracts have valid purpose.

These instruments have, however, become convoluted and corrupted by greedy interests that wish to make a quick fortune without doing anything useful to earn their fortune. As investors push stock prices higher with their frantic purchasing, they draw in other opportunistic investors who also trade to make a profit on the rising prices. These traders are generating money by circulating it through trading mechanisms and getting rich. They stay at the sharp end of inflation because they push rapidly changing prices to their limit and cause their money and their markets to grow as fast as the money and credit supply will allow. Prices have the capacity to increase to the degree that there are dollars available to buy them. When money and credit are released into the system those that increase their prices the fastest to take advantage of that fattened money supply make money out of nothing. The Wall Street markets have become simply a means to rapidly inflate trading prices so as to take advantage of that mechanism of inflation.

Pure speculation on the price of anything is an errant practice. The value of anything and everything can be calculated according to standardized measurements. Leaving the value of economic assets open to arbitrary speculation leaves those controlling the propaganda and money flow to do what they will with the economy and its hard-earned assets. And, predictably, what they invariably do with the economy is move money and assets into their own holdings.

The less tangible the item being traded, the more the value can be inflated and the more money can be made. Witness the currency and financial derivative markets.

Currency trading for profit is virtually criminal. No worthwhile production occurs and great masses of money are sucked out of national economies. Again, speculating on the value of something which has a calculable value is like betting on the weight of a dog—entertaining, perhaps, but certainly not productive. And those that make the biggest killing on the currency markets have already weighed the dog; they have the inside scoop on which currencies are being most heavily subjected to inflation and which ones aren't. It would be funny if it wasn't looting national economies and the pockets of productive, hardworking people.

The derivatives markets amount to placing bets on other bets already made. It is yet another market that is very loosely tied to anything tangible and so can have its prices more readily inflated. It is yet another vehicle to ride the wave of inflation on.

If it were possible to calculate the amount of money made in capital gains by those playing the various financial sector markets, you would be looking at the amount of money that could be poured right back into the economy and into the hands of productive people. It is suffice to say that the banking and finance institutions occupy the largest office towers in your nearest big city. It is the richest part of society while also being the least productive and most dysfunctional. There is immense social advance to be made in dissolving this speculative trading industry alone.

Insurance

Another monstrous leech squirming around in the banking and financial industry is the insurance business. Insurance companies make money simply because accidents, illness and injury occur. Accidents are going to happen. But there is absolutely no rational justification for private companies to make obscene profits because of the fact.

Furthermore, it is asking for trouble to allow profit to be made on accidents, illness and injury—it simply promotes the occurrence of such. Even short of blatant insurance fraud, broad social incentive to reduce the likelihood and impact of accident and illness is successfully discouraged when powerful industries are dependent upon the occurrence of such.

Using insurance companies to absorb the impact and shock of accident and disaster repair costs is bad enough, but when government legislation enforces it, you really are headed down an ugly road. Yes, people need help when misfortune strikes. But people should not have to fight for legitimate claims and they most certainly should not need to pay insurance premiums to greedy, profit-hungry insurance companies to protect themselves.

When you conceive of the profits made in the insurance business, you are looking at another staggering volume of money that is being extorted from the productive person's economy, and that could be flowing through your own productive hands, instead of into the greedy and manipulative bankers' coffers.

THE SOLUTION: EXCHANGE TIME

The Essential Element

In introducing Social Viability's commercial policies, the first thing that must be dealt with is the currency used. Social Viability does not sanction the use of the dollar or the pound or any other national currency in use today. These elastic currencies are corrupted and manipulated by those who work to economically enslave the productive people of the world.

To begin with, we need to step back and look at the fundamental purpose of money and determine the essential element that constitutes the value of a product or service. Later we will apply that to a system of exchange able to function in a modern economy.

The fundamental purpose of money is to facilitate cooperative effort; to aid the interaction of producers and consumers in an advanced society. It allows people to readily exchange their own products and services for the products and services of others in society. A carpenter works skillfully at his specialized trade and receives money in return. He can use that money to hire a painter to paint his house. If he were to take time away from his own trade, go out and learn the trade of painting, gain the experience and purchase the necessary equipment to paint his house and then do a good job of it himself, it would take a relatively long time. If he simply works in the trade he is familiar with and equipped to do, and is paid fairly as a carpenter, he can exchange the work he does as a carpenter for the work of the painter and he can have the job finished in much shorter order.

Money allows civilized man to get much more accomplished by eliminating the need for clumsy barter, allowing people to trade highly specialized products and services. It's all about increased productivity through division of labor as Adam Smith explained it in *The Wealth of Nations*. One man manufactures cars, another man builds houses, another bakes bread, another tailors clothes, and through the use of money everyone can have a car, a comfortable home, good food to eat, and quality clothing on their back. If each man had to do all of these things alone or barter crudely, most of us would still be riding horses, living in shacks with dirt floors, eating the same food all of the time and wearing rags.

I have heard it said that money is the root of all evil. It is not. It is often mistakenly thought so merely because money is as useful in working evil deeds as it is in building civilizations. The materialistic greed centered on money compels many an evil deed, but the truth is that money is merely a tool. An axe is a very useful tool in chopping wood for the fireplace that will keep your family warm. It is also a very useful tool in a psychotic, bloodthirsty effort to kill and maim.

Money is, in fact, a vital element in civilized social activity. It is, however, very misunderstood. The thing that is most misunderstood, or most overlooked, about money is what its essential element is.

Time is money. It has become an oft used cliché. It is simple. But it is true. The essential element of money is time in terms of human labor. This is crucial to understand fully because all of the convoluted aberrations surrounding money in today's culture stem from having lost sight of this fact. It is the reason we have such vague and varying tools—such as dollars, pounds, yen or euros—for measuring the value of economic goods and services.

We cannot go on valuing our goods and services with dollars and cents that themselves have no defined value. One of the units in the measurement of distance is the meter. One can say something is so many meters long, and if someone asks, "exactly how long is that?" there are various standards including a bar with marks on it that exactly define its length—no grey area. Clear definitions such as this are the foundations that allow sciences to function, intricate developments to be made, and advanced technologies to be codified.

When referring to economic value, one can say that something costs so many dollars, and if someone asks, "exactly how valuable is that?" one could only reply with a reference to some other currency which defines itself against another currency etc., etc. "A meter is about three feet and a foot is about one third of a meter," and it goes back and forth and no one ever gets out an actual ruler and says, "It's this long." One could say,

"A dollar is approximately equal to two cans of soda." But that changes from store to store, city to city, nation to nation. "A meter is about this long," says someone with their hands spaced apart. Fine unless you want to measure exact distances needed for intricate applications. Let's see a builder construct a modern structure with a series of "about-this-longs" instead of a tape measure and transit.

If a builder could not build large, intricate structures without exactly defined measuring standards, how do we expect to build large, intricate economies with its measuring standards constantly changing, different from one day to the next and never actually defined? The ability to readily measure value of products and services is crucial to our efforts to build viable economies.

It is essential that we keep in view the fact that money— that units of currency—must represent useful goods and services when used in transactions. Bankers sell the use of the currency and the money represents itself and not a real commodity. It is a corruption of its use and encumbers any economy in which the practice is allowed. Any efforts to establish genuine economic health are in vain if the abolition of this system of banking is not the highest priority.

This brings us inevitably back to the subject of how to determine the value of a currency. What benchmark or basic unit is to be used to measure useful goods and services? We need a basic measurement with which all products or services can be measured in regards to their actual economic value.

At this point it must be stressed that we are referring to value in an economic term, quite apart from the concept of importance. High-tech equipment is costly—it has relatively high value. However, it is not important when compared with food, water and breathable air. These things are usually either quite cheap or free of charge altogether. They are most important, but generally of minimal economic value.

Again, the datum that is either brushed off as a cliché or not seriously taught at all is: *TIME IS MONEY.*

The fundamental unit of measurement for economic value is time in human labor. It is that simple. Goods and services that require a lot of time in their construction and/or delivery are of high value. The single basic element that sets apart the value of a motor vehicle from the value of an apple is the time invested in its creation or acquisition by people. Market factors such as supply and demand are outdated and clumsy ways in which to determine the value and hence price of any commodity. The meter is not defined by how much timber you need to build a home. Such market conditions can be and often are manipulated deliberately and have no place exerting determination over prices in a fair and viable economy. Once upon a time, there was no other way to price goods and services. Times have now changed.

The sole factor is time in human labor for determining the actual economic value of a product or service, and that is the basic unit of currency in Social Viability's commercial policies.

A loaf of bread would be priced in terms of minutes, a simple piece of furniture in hours, and a motor vehicle in terms of weeks or perhaps months. When you work, you are paid for the hours you work and you can then take those hours in your account and use them to buy the things you need and want.

The training required to perform your job is built into the hours you perform on the job, and hence the amount you are paid. A laborer that does not require any formal training to perform his job would be recompensed only for the hours put in on the job. A technician who undertook formal training would have the time he took to train built into the hours he works and so would be paid for his hours at work plus an additional compensation for his time in training. The amount of training compensation depends upon how much formal training was taken.

These commercial policies represent the most efficient and effective means of running an economy. Using modern computer and communication technologies, hitherto unforeseen prosperity may be achieved in modern economies. However, the success of such hinges upon the use of a measurable, calculable trade currency that can be used to precisely monitor and manage these modern intricate economies.

Value Stability

Using Social Viability's commercial policies, prices are simply calculated rather than arbitrarily set, negotiated over or bid upon. Underpricing as well as overpricing is prevented. This is important since underpricing is used dishonestly by powerful companies to put other honest vendors and producers out of business. It is often just as detrimental and underhanded as over-pricing goods and services because it is done so as to cull opposition and gain the opportunity to over-price.

The entire operation of the commercial services needs to revolve around the principle of making economic transactions a mechanism that allows production to build wealth for individuals and societies. In today's world transactions are themselves a means to build wealth. Buying low and selling high without any useful contribution does nothing more than draw wealth away from those that do provide useful service and production. Such a system disproportionately rewards the slick merchants and traders. Merchants and traders should be paid for efficiently providing the valuable service they do provide, not for taking advantage of commercial situations that have nothing to do with the actual value of the products for sale.

On the other hand, measurable pricing offers a system that rewards the innovative and productive—the people upon whose back civilization rides. Honest producers should be able to count on a stable and valid pricing mechanism that guarantees fair remuneration for their time and effort.

Social Viability, then, needs a currency format that uses time in human labor as a basis for price calculation of products and services. Calculation of price is achieved by simply calculating the time taken to produce and deliver the product or service. The currency used for this purpose is known as *Exchange Time*.

There are two basic units of Exchange Time: years and days. Years are shown with the symbol, Ŧ. Days are shown with the symbol, ŧ. Years are broken down into subunits of weeks. A price of two years, twenty weeks is shown as Ŧ2:20. Days are broken down into subunits of degrees—360 degrees. Degrees are used as a more convenient subdivision of days because there are too few hours in a day and too many minutes in a day to be practical in pricing. For relative comparison, one degree is equal to four minutes and there are fifteen degrees in an hour. A price of five days, one hundred and fifty degrees is shown as ŧ5:150. Small prices of degrees or fractions of a degree can also be shown with the symbol, °. A price of one-half of a degree can be shown as ŧ0:0.5 or ŧ.5°

To give some idea of relative value, on the next page are some comparisons between Exchange Time and US Dollars. The conversion is based on $14.15/hour, the median hourly wage for employed persons in the United States as of May, 2006 according to the US Dept of Labor, Bureau of Labor Statistics.

ŧ0:1 = 94¢

ŧ1:00 = $339.60

Ŧ0:1 = $2,377.20

Ŧ1:0 = $123,614.40

1¢ = ŧ0: 0.01 or ŧ.01°

25¢ = ŧ0: 0.27 or ŧ.27°

$1.00 = ŧ0: 1.06 or ŧ1.06°

$50.00 = ŧ0: 53.00 or ŧ53.00°

$1,000 = ŧ2: 340.07

$10,000 = ŧ29:160.71

$100,000 = ŧ294:167.07 or Ŧ0: 42.07

$1million = Ŧ8:05

$1billion = Ŧ8089:35

$1trillion = Ŧ8,089,672:21

You will notice that Exchange Time units include quite large denominations. It is designed to make calculations of social volumes of trade less cumbersome to deal with. It has greater room for expanded orders of magnitude in volume of trade than does the dollar or other common currencies, but at the same time can be used for very small amounts.

Calculating the price of an item is simple in concept, but there are a number of factors that must be taken into account in doing so to reach a fair and accurate figure.

Let's take the practical example of a baker and an assistant spending two hours to make and sell sixty loaves of bread. Two people spending two hours makes a total of four hours spent. Four hours equals sixty degrees of exchange time. Sixty degrees divided by sixty loaves equals one degree, or t0:1 per loaf. This is the *labor component* of the price.

Let's say the cost of the ingredients to make the twenty loaves of bread also totaled sixty degrees, or t0:60. This amount divided among all of the loaves of bread would equal an additional t0:1 per loaf. This is the *substance component* of the price.

Also we must incorporate the cost of the tools, energy and other consumables used in the process. This includes the cost of the machinery, such as the oven; the cost of the kitchen implements used in the process; and the cost of the electricity or gas to power the oven. In calculating the inclusive cost of an oven, for example, let's say the oven cost ŧ5:00 and that such ovens average a life span of five years, and that in five years an oven will bake one hundred thousand loaves of bread. ŧ5:00 divided by one hundred thousand equals eighteen thousandths of a degree or ŧ.018° per loaf of bread. If this amount plus all other such incidental costs equaled ŧ.1° then this would be added to the price of the bread as the *materiel component* of the price.

A basic price calculation for a loaf of bread would look like this:

Value Component	Amount
Labor	ŧ0:1
Substance	ŧ0:1
Materiel	ŧ0:0.1
Total Price:	ŧ0:2.1

There is another type of product that involves more factors in its price calculation. It is the *multiple consumer product*.

A multiple consumer product (or MCP) is a commodity or service that, as a finished product, may be purchased by more than one consumer.

An apple is not an MCP. It is grown, its price is calculated, it is sold at that price and it is consumed by the buyer.

An example of an MCP would be a motion picture. The product is consumed by any number of people. Other examples of MCPs would be storybooks, software programs and musical compositions. Many art forms are MCPs.

As an example of how to calculate pricing for MCPs, let's say that a motion picture has its production cost calculated at Ŧ500. The production cost is calculated in the same manner as any single consumption product—like the loaf of bread. Obviously, it would be incorrect to price a single movie ticket at Ŧ500. This would be more than anyone would make in a lifetime and any single ticket would cover the entire production cost. The production cost should be divided among them to arrive at the price of a single ticket.

After the production cost is calculated, the next factor that needs to be weighed in is that of the median number of people that watch any given film. Let's say in this example that over the year prior to the film's release, the median consumption was ten million ticket sales per film for that type of production.

The production cost is divided by the median consumption to arrive at the consumption price, Ŧ0:6.57. If the film is popular and draws ticket sales greater than the median consumption of ten million, the owners will be rewarded with a return greater than the investment of time and labor. If the film draws a below-average number of ticket sales, their return will not be favorable. Good works are rewarded with wealth, and vise versa, as it should be. High quality as well as efficient production are promoted and rewarded at the same time.

Here is a basic price calculation for the motion picture example:

Value Component	Amount
Labor	Ŧ400
Substance	Ŧ15
Materiel	Ŧ85
Production Cost:	Ŧ500
Median Consumption	10,000,000
Consumption Price:	ŧ0:6.57

The value of any product or service can be quite easily calculated using these policies and the Exchange Time currency. With such a system of exchange, all values can be accurately calculated and economies can be stabilized. Depressions, recessions, inflation and chronic economic fluctuation can be brought under control and even eliminated altogether.

Strong houses can be built using a tape measure and a transit. Strong economies that don't crash and fluctuate can be built using Social Viability's commercial policies and the currency, Exchange Time.

Credit Loans

First and foremost, the usurious practices of the banking industry have no part whatsoever in Social Viability commercial policies. There is no interest charged on any loan for any purpose. Beyond simple administrative fees for the record keeping of loans and their repayment, there are no additional costs; no payment of monies over and above the repayment of the loan itself.

Loans are managed as a matter of public interest rather than used as an avenue for personal profit. When new money is introduced into an economy through a loan to some person or business, the loan is effectively extended by the entire economy. Granting money to someone before they have contributed something of worth to society devalues everyone's money because the amount of currency is being increased in relation to the productivity that is occurring. That's what inflation is. As the person uses the loan to generate more commercial activity, productivity increases to meet the increased currency in circulation. The loan should, therefore, be repaid to all of society, collectively. Everyone's money is affected by the extension of loans so it should be done on behalf of everyone that uses a given currency.

The only time inflation is not incurred by extending loans is if someone loans money they have saved, rather than new money being introduced into the economy to lend. This does not induce inflation because the money has already come into circulation and been saved by someone. However, using one's saved money as a commodity with which to generate more wealth is still a perversion of the mechanism. If one has monetary capital they would like to put to use, they may loan it to or invest it in a commercial enterprise, but they may not charge interest on the loan or collect gains that exceed the value of their investment.

"Where, then, is the incentive for someone to make loans or invest in commercial activity?" one may ask. It is a valid and important question. Firstly, investors will be awarded a share of the social investment fund (more on this later). Also, those that invest their wealth back into society are rewarded with an increase in citizen rank which affords one several advantages.

Furthermore, specific business incentives will exist.   For example, a businessman operating a manufacturing plant may loan money to a company that is building a rail line that will open up a whole new market for his manufactured wares. He will not collect interest on the loan, but he will enjoy the expansion of his business into the new market that the rail line opens up to him. Furthermore, the citizen rank that is awarded to him for investing in another business will put him in better stead in an application for a loan to expand his manufacturing facility.

When specific commercial interests such as this form a part of the incentive, investment of money is more closely tied to actual social benefits and productive results. If an investor's sole incentive is a financial capital gain, all manner of perverted results not necessarily tied to real productivity can ensue. Rather than investment in a rail line which advances infrastructure and actually benefits society, when capital gains are the sole incentive, you find investment in things like pharmaceutical companies that can generate handsome profits due to securing a patent on some drug, but whose activities actually promote ill health and weakness in society.

Loans made in any form advance the economy that everyone relies on for their well-being. It is crucial that these loans be tied to real social benefit, rather than individual greed and opportunism. That is not to say that someone should not lend funds or take out a loan to forward their own interests. It is to say that the system in which loans are made should be formulated in such a way as to encourage lending for productive and benevolent purposes.

Also, the system should guard against overreaching a society's resources. While lending is an excellent vehicle for expanding economic activity, it can also wreak havoc if mismanaged. As an economic safety precaution, the amount of loaned credit outstanding in any given economic system must be kept to a certain percentage of the economic activity occurring.

The total volume of Exchange Time transacted in a given period is the standard against which you measure the safe volume of outstanding loaned credit. This is the *power* of an economy— its transaction volume per given time period.

The *loan extension rate* is applied to the power to calculate the *loan extension limit* which is the total volume of Exchange Time that can be outstanding in loans not yet repaid.

If, in a given society, the power is calculated at ₮20 per month and the loan extension rate is 5%, then the loan extension limit will be ₮1, i.e. no more than ₮1 should be outstanding in loans not yet repaid for the following month. The purpose is to ensure that loans of new money are absorbed by the economic turnover of the rest of society without undue economic disruption. If ₮20 per month are transacted in an economy and ₮18 are outstanding in loans, and if a large number of debtors decide to spend all at once, the economy will be consumed. There will not be enough goods and services to go around.

Its *strength* is the total Exchange Time on account for an entire economy—all the money that all account holders have saved. The loan extension rate must be raised and lowered in relation to the growth and contraction of the strength of the economy.

An economy's strength represents its capacity to absorb losses. If there is a great volume of Exchange Time saved in members' accounts, then they have worked many hours, contributed much and that productivity is now in the hands of other buyers in the society as real and usable goods and results. This means there is material and financial wealth people can rely upon and dip into.

An economy's power represents how quickly it will recover from losses. If there is not much commercial transaction occurring, there is not much active production going on. People may be content and have most of what they need so they work little and do not trade much. This means that the commercial activity is minimal. If a substantial loss were incurred, the active economic momentum needed to rapidly replace the losses would not exist. The workforce may be present but dormant, and it would take some time to gather everyone together and organize them to recover the economic losses, whereas if the power was high—if there was a great deal of production and output—a loss would be quickly replaced.

And that is how loaned credit must be viewed: as a loss for the entire society, even if merely a temporary one. Goods and services are being consumed without prior contribution. This consumption must be absorbed without impacting the satisfaction of the supply demands of the society at large.

If there is a great deal of strength in an economy and it is very powerful, then a relatively high percentage of that vast power may be loaned out without undue risk. If there is equally great strength present but a reduced power—reduced transaction activity—the percentage will be just as high, but it will be a percentage of a lower economic power and will mean less credit will be loaned out. If there is a low level of strength but a high rate of transaction, then a lower percentage will be applied to a higher economic power figure to determine the amount of loaned credit to be made available.

Example: an economy has a strength of ₮500 and a power of ₮10 transacted per month. The strength of ₮500 prompts the loan extension rate to be set at, let's say, 5%. 5% of ₮10 gives a loan extension limit of ₮0:26, so in any given month the amount of outstanding spendable credit should not exceed ₮0:26. This means that if there is already T0:20 in outstanding loans not yet repaid, no more than T0:6 should be extended in new loans.

If the power rating for that society increases to T12 transacted per month, the loan extension limit would be raised to T0:31.2 (5% of T12). If the strength then lowered to T450, perhaps prompting a reduction of the loan extension limit to 4%, the credit limit would be reduced to T0:24.96 (4% of T12).

The next issue to consider in the granting of credit loans is to whom the loans are extended. If the social loan extension limit is greater than the aggregate of all loans applied for, then this issue is null and void. All applications for loans to members in good standing would be granted.

If, however, there are more applications for loans than credit allowable, the following priorities are followed:

The highest priorities are *emergency loans*. These loans supplant the profit reaping insurance industry and effectively fully insure everyone in a viable society against all possible accident and illness. These types of loans must be granted as a matter of priority and are the only grounds for the social loan extension limit to be violated. In this case, all other loans would be suspended until the outstanding loans were again brought to within the social loan extension limit.

Emergency loans would be granted to all suffering loss of property due to natural disaster or accident, and anyone suffering from loss of health due to illness or accident. Emergency loans must be granted promptly so that peoples' lives may be returned to normal as quickly as possible. Note: these are loans. They must be repaid. They are repaid interest free, but they are repaid nonetheless. Those that have a lot of accidents and get sick often will have to pay the bills. They will be covered and insured against disaster, but they need to pay what is due sooner or later. Those with outstanding emergency loans are ineligible for any other loans until their emergency loans are repaid.

If, for example, someone's home is destroyed by fire, they are granted an emergency loan to rebuild. If they are charged no interest, only paying simple administrative fees, then they can get their lives back on track without superfluous expense. They will have never have had to pay any home insurance premiums during their entire home-owning lives, and will be paying only for the damage incurred. And those that manage to prevent their homes from ever being set ablaze or damaged in any way will never need to pay a red cent in extortionate home insurance. They will be able to use that money to help educate their children, start new enterprises and provide for their families.

If someone's reckless or careless driving causes a car wreck, then they would pay for the damage to the vehicles and people involved. If unable to afford it, they would have an emergency loan taken in their name to pay for the damage. Everyone's property would be repaired or replaced immediately and the culprit would pay off the loan which paid for the destruction caused. Those that never cause a traffic accident would never have to pay a penny in vehicle insurance premiums which, for safe drivers, amount to payments that cover the costs of accidents caused by other people.

Those that cause accidents should foot the bill. People should pay for the repairs to their own property when no one in particular or Mother Nature is the culprit in an accident. Such policy promotes the protection and safeguarding of one's own property. To make everyone pay premiums so as to cover the expenses of the accident-prone and clumsy (not to mention perpetrators of insurance fraud), as well as the expensive lives of insurance company executives is ludicrous.

The next priorities in the granting of loans are *enterprise loans*. These are for loans to start or expand businesses. This is of high priority because it is business enterprises that will expand the economic capacity and scope of the society. Business enterprises constitute the engine that powers the economy so this must constitute the priority investment of loaned credit after emergency loans.

The lowest priorities are *personal loans*. These are for personal effects not of a crucial or emergency nature. They are granted only when there are no other demands from the first two priorities. But they are granted without credit check, lists of references, guarantors or anything else. There will be restrictions placed on those that have outstanding loans, especially when those loans are not being repaid in a timely manner, but they will not have to pay interest on those loans.

The next factor to take into account when granting credit loans is citizen rank. All loan applications of equal priority level are granted based on these grounds (except for emergency loans which are granted to everyone regardless of rank where there is a genuine, urgent need). Citizen rank is earned through contribution to society. Those of higher rank are granted loans first, and then on down the list until the social loan extension limit is reached. This is important because social strength and stability depends upon those that contribute much being rewarded with privileges for their efforts. To deny rewards to strong contributors is to remove encouragement to excel in the construction of civilization.

The granting of loans is an integral part of building social economic prosperity. It gives people a kick-start in their commercial and personal endeavors while generating economic activity that benefits everyone. It expands the real productive economy and expands the money supply to match.

And that brings us to a crucial subject: the management of the expansion of the money supply. Too great a money supply—a volume of currency that expands faster than the productive economy—invokes inflation and instability. Too short a money supply—a stagnant or shrinking volume of currency that does not keep up with the productive economy— retards economic activity.

Currently, central banks invent money, say it is theirs and then loan it out. This expands the money supply. However, they do it at too high a rate and this inevitably creates the problem of over-inflated currencies. The US dollar is a perfect example. The Federal Reserve banks make a colossal fortune when they inflate the currency. All of the money they electronically print is claimed as their own. They get richer right away. Then they lend this money they invented and are paid interest on it. They get richer still. In short, they have a massive vested interest in inflating the currency. The more they inflate it, the richer they get.

Conversely, during the Middle Ages in Europe there was a shortage of money. The economic activity was stifled and the general poverty was a result. When the Spanish discovered the gold and silver in the Americas and brought it back, the money supply expanded (in gold and silver coinage) and the Industrial Revolution ensued.

Social Viability commercial policy expands the money supply with the productive economy thus:

1. Loans are made according to the formulae outlined earlier. This is new money that does not exist in any reserves anywhere. Any loan made by a private individual or business with their own reserves is a different matter altogether.

2. When these loans are repaid, the money goes into a *social investment fund* which is then periodically dispersed to those that have invested in the economy. Any person or business that employs labor, that leases property, or that invests their finances with private loans or stock purchases is considered an *economic investor* and will be awarded with a share of the social investment fund. The share received by each economic investor will be proportionate to how much they invest in the economy.

Instead of the criminals of today's central banks claiming the new money that enters into the economy as their own, the productive business owners, landowners and investors will be rewarded. New money will not be exploited by those who commit usury; it will be employed by those who build higher standards of living for us all.

The Economics of Production

Just as all prices for all goods and services are calculated on the basis of simple equations, so are employees' wages.

The base wage for all employees is ŧ0:15 per hour. This means that for every hour an employee works, they are paid an hour of Exchange Time. Remember, one day of Exchange Time—ŧ1:0—is divided up into three hundred and sixty degrees. ŧ1:0 = ŧ0:360. There are twenty-four hours in a day, 15 degrees—ŧ0:15—per hour. If a person works for an hour, they get paid for an hour. If a person works eight hours, they get paid for what amounts to eight hours in Exchange Time: ŧ0:120.

If a person has undergone specialized, unpaid training off the job in order to acquire education and/or training necessary to the profession, they will also have a professional remuneration built into their wage.

For example, if a prospective engineer undertakes education and training that costs ŧ80, then the professional remuneration will spread the cost of his education and training into his income throughout the span of a *career term* of five years. If the engineer works in that profession full-time (forty hours per week) for five full years, he will be fully remunerated for those education and training expenses. If one works full time, fifty-two weeks per year for five years, one will have worked ten thousand, four hundred hours. If the ŧ80 in training costs are spread over this time, the engineer will earn an extra t0:2.77 per hour which is added to the base wage.

This wage does not get adjusted at the end of the career term. If a person remains in the profession beyond the five-year career term, they continue to earn the professional remuneration credit as an incentive to remain in the field in which they are trained and experienced. If the engineer leaves his profession before reaching the career term, he will personally bear the balance of the cost of the education and training.

If someone sells products or provides service as an independent sole proprietor, rather than as a part of a company, then they will sell the goods at their calculated price with the base wage (plus any professional remuneration) included in the labor component of the price calculation.

In a company that employs the time of others, the labor of all employees is used in the calculation of the labor component of the price of the products or services delivered.

The substance and materiel components of the price of the sold products return funds to the owners and investors that supplied the capital that bought the raw materials, supplies and equipment. If an owner or shareholder works at a company as well as having capital invested in it, they must be paid for their time in their day-to-day working capacity in addition to any return they collect on their investment of capital.

Going back to our baker example, let's say in this case that the owner of the small bakery takes no part in the business operations.   There are only two employees: a baker and an assistant. In a single day, the baker and his assistant bake and sell sixty loaves of bread. They each work an eight hour day, use ŧ0:60 in ingredients and use ŧ5 in materiel costs.

Price Calculation for 60 loaves of bread:

Value Component	Amount
Labor	ŧ0:240
Substance	ŧ0:60
Materiel	ŧ0:5
Total Price:	ŧ0:305
Per Loaf:	ŧ0:5.08

In this case, the labor component of the bread sold would be used to pay the baker and his assistant for their time spent on the job.   The substance and materiel components would reimburse the owner for the ingredients that he bought and materiel that he supplied his employees with.

If, in a different scenario, the baker was the sole owner of the business, working daily in the business he owned, he would collect his ŧ120 share of the labor component as well as the ingredient and materiel components.

If an investor helped the baker purchase some of the equipment to get the business started, the shareholder would be paid a dividend from the substance and/or the materiel components. If, for example, the shareholder invested ŧ20 in the equipment when the business opened in return for a 50% share in the materiel costs, then he would receive ŧ0:2.5 from that day's business. He would continue to receive the dividend—the 50% cut of the materiel costs—until he had been recompensed for the full ŧ20 that he originally invested. At ŧ0:2.5 per day, it would be about eleven years before the full investment was paid back.

Someone who thought like a banker would argue that the investor made no profit from his investment in the bakery. He invested ŧ20 and was repaid ŧ20 over eleven years. It was nothing more than an interest-free loan.

This is true. However, the investor is now going to receive a share of the social investment fund. The investor is literally going to be given money as a reward for being an economic investor which will provide ample personal incentive.

Also, there is the additional incentive to make capital investments due to the benefits of increased citizenship ranking which generates such advantages as higher qualification for new loans. It could be likened to a credit rating which is based not on repaying loans taken out by oneself, but rather on making loans to others.

Not to forget, the investor will also have the dividend coming in as residual income. Creditors will provide for themselves a steady, if small, income flowing in for a long period of time. There is no devaluation of the currency through inflation so the amount invested will really be the amount repaid. The repayment of a loan in the amount of the original loan in an inflationary economy is actually a loss. Using Social Viability's commercial policies, there is no such inflation—no chronic devaluation of the currency—and no such loss.

With this arrangement, the price of goods is vastly reduced for everyone compared with what we know today in this banker-infested economy. As the cost of living and the cost of doing business drops, that frantic, desperate scramble to increase profits is relieved.

Using such a system and the Exchange Time currency, all costs in terms of time in human labor are passed on to the consumer by the producers and service providers. Money enters into the economy with the economic investors and it is carried through by way of simple calculation at every step of the economic process. Consumers pay for exactly what they consume. Producers are paid fairly for the work they perform. And investors buy themselves an income for a time without having to profit unfairly on the labor of others while being rewarded for their contribution to the expansion of the economy. Opportunism, profiteering, usury and hostile business practices are nullified. Investment in the productive economy is rewarded and the entrepreneurial spirit is encouraged.

All of the convoluted manipulations used to manage (and exploit) economic activity melt away when the fundamental processes used for the essential function of the system are based on workable principles. Economics as a subject has been made complicated as authorities sought to compensate for its fundamental shortcomings (which can be said for any subject that ties itself in knots and doesn't really get anywhere). Economics is actually very simple in concept, even if it gets involved with its dimensions and calculations.

When sound methodology is put to use, only then can economics become focused on production and innovation rather than on inflation, interest rates and synthetic market trends; only then can the entrepreneurs, inventors and efficient producers surpass the bankers and politicians in importance and wealth; and only then can society at large enjoy broad prosperity as those that genuinely create quality of life for everyone get their just rewards.

Shareholding & Incorporation

Incorporation is an uncomplicated process in Social Viability and has broad applicability. Any member or group of members can form a corporation. The purpose is simply to create an entity that can have its own account, apply for loans and function as a separate entity from any single person. There are no legal protections afforded under a corporation. Social Viability justice policies are such that one need not protect oneself from the law or frivolous civil suits.

A person can start a business on their own and incorporate that business so it has its own account, even if they are a sole proprietor. A group of people can pool resources, issue shares and form a corporation to do business. A marriage is simply a familial incorporation and follows much the same system and guidelines.

With Social Viability, provisions exist for the ownership of shares in an enterprise. There are several major differences in the arrangement of the system, however, compared with what exists in the stock markets of today.

Firstly, as with any other product or service in the economy, business enterprises, themselves, have a calculable value. The value of a business enterprise is calculated by adding all of the time invested into the development and establishment of the business—termed *labor value*—to the cost of all purchased wherewithal that is owned by the company—known as *property value*. This provides a price that the company itself can be bought and sold for.

Shares owned by investors may be traded for the value of the outstanding investment that has not been repaid through dividends. There is no avenue for capital gains on an investment in Social Viability. A stock investment is a vehicle used to generate a dividend income for a time and to claim a share of the social investment fund. Nothing more. No gambling. No day trading. No artificial stock value inflation.

One of the most basic tenets of Social Viability commercial policy is: **Productivity and contribution, alone, call for financial remuneration.**

Those that live idle, opulent lives through avenues that contribute nothing to society at large will protest violently against such policy. Such protests speak loudly: "Please don't make me actually work to earn my keep! I am quite satisfied living and leeching off the works of others!"

Social Viability's commercial policies guarantee greater living conditions for productive people simply because those that contribute valued products and useful services will be rewarded with wealth. The idle leisure class, the greedy traders and criminal bankers that drain wealth from the greater society will finally be eradicated.

CHAPTER 3
WORTHY LEADERS

THE PROBLEM: DEMOCRATIC GOVERNMENT

The Illusion of Freedom

M ANY living under democratic governments today believe that being given the choice between two or three candidates in an election grants one freedom. This is widely believed primarily because politicians and media talking heads say it a lot. They have a vested interest in people believing in democracy and often people who are especially afraid of enslavement will insist that they are free despite the most glaring contrary evidence. Slaves that believe themselves to be free are much less troublesome.

If all of the candidates offered up for election are chosen by, and answerable to, a cabal of plutocratic tyrants, are the people free? If your options are dictated to you by your enemy, are you safe?

Democracy was always doomed to eventual failure based on simple analysis. Public office is occupied by those who win the most votes according to some electoral system or another. To be able to vote for a candidate, people must first know that a candidate exists and then have information about them upon which to base a decision, regardless of how simplistic or emotional it is. Therefore, political candidates need exposure. Exposure costs money in advertising—these days hundreds of millions of dollars for the highest offices. That money comes from election campaign contributors. The rich men who contribute to election campaigns expect results from their candidates if elected, and the candidates either clearly understand this or just happen to be mindlessly predisposed to support the agenda of the contributing master. Politicians, then, are effectively in the employ of the super-wealthy that supply the funds that get them elected.

A politician must establish early in his career an adherence to the agenda of the political funding clique or he will never gain the backing required to reach any degree of political success.

You do what your boss tells you to do because he pays you. The same goes with a politician. Actually, the fact that your boss pays you is what makes him your boss. To delude oneself into believing that the general populace is the elected leaders' bosses or that our politicians don't have bosses to answer to is naive.

So the figureheads we see on television are not our ultimate leaders? Then who are? And who selects them?

The ease with which democracies can be subverted is relative to the prevalence of mass communication media. The more people that can be communicated to at once, the more people's ideas and opinions can be manipulated with high-volume, dynamic, emotionally stirring propaganda. And today, more than ever, we have those media.

Democracy was an attempt to take the power from the rich ruling elite and give it to the people at large because, historically, monarchs and dictators could be counted on to abuse their power. In a time when radio, television and the internet did not exist, democracy had a fighting chance of functioning as it was intended. Unfortunately, as time has gone by and as communications technologies have developed, all that has resulted is the facade that the people hold the power while, in reality, we are mere subjects of yet another generation of the ruling elite that is continuing with the same sordid brand of behavior. In some respects today's democracy is worse than a dictatorship or monarchy because the ultimate rulers can hide behind puppets and keep their faces and true motives out of sight, making the tyranny all the more difficult to identify and overcome.

Taxation

Taxation is most the commonly accepted method for pooling social funds. People may not like it, but they accept it. Taxation is not a direct payment for a specific service. You are forced under threat of imprisonment to pay a percentage of your income and of the money you spend on certain goods to the government. When all is said and done, probably close to half of the money you earn goes to the government in the United States. Most of that money disappears into the nebulous federal budget and comes out in all manner of deranged spending. It is virtually impossible to track where all of your taxed earnings are being spent. You are not notified of how your money is being spent. The research required to find out how all of your tax dollars are being spent is far too tedious to make the effort worthwhile. The government is not held to account for its spending—after all, who can hold them to account? The voters who haven't much hope of ever finding out exactly how their money is actually spent?

The federal government in the United States spends appalling volumes of money in a plethora of foolish endeavors. The taxpayers are forking over deplorable proportions of their earnings to politicians to be spent in deplorable ways.

The amount of economic relief that would be experienced if government spending was brought into a sane realm is enormous. And the system that feeds it is the taxation system that is but a tool of the despot.

Legislation

The legislative branch of government in the United States along with its counterparts in other parts of the world are yet more examples of accepted institutions that, when examined objectively, are utterly absurd. That people accept institutions that seem bent on enslaving them simply because they have been long since established is a great shame.

The legislative branch of government makes up and enacts laws. The legislators make up laws their bosses (the election campaign contributors) want enacted. Thus, the extremely wealthy effectively make the laws. These laws tell us how to behave when living, working, socializing and trading with others. The laws that our enlightened lords make up for us dictate right and wrong to us—or at least attempt to.

Now, I'm well aware of the difference between right and wrong. I'm quite certain that you are too. Any three-year-old knows what is right and what is wrong. It is a part of our innate nature. To presume that we need a bunch of bought politicians to determine for us what we already understand is demented.

When excessive numbers of laws are passed, especially when those laws become too numerous to memorize, too complex to understand and are often contradictory to the very principles of right and wrong, people are inclined to feel encouraged to violate natural law and do the wrong thing just as a matter of protest. The more oppressed a man, the more likely he will rebel against authority—even if the rebellion results in further degradation of himself.

Legislation is a self-perpetuating aberration. The passing of onerous and needless laws creates an atmosphere of oppression. Those feeling the worst of the oppression rebel and break the law; sometimes out of desperation and sometimes just for the sake of breaking the law. These people often get trapped in a vicious circle that spirals out of control and results in truly harmful and atrocious acts. Those at the top of the legislative food chain can then convincingly pronounce, "Look at how unlawful and criminally inclined people are!" People have no argument for this and support the insanity that is the endless legislation of new laws.

Furthermore, laws are rarely retired. New laws and amendments are being dreamt up and enacted continually. Thus, laws continue to stack up in volume and complexity to the point where few are aware of the details of the intricate and involved laws that they are supposed to obey. One must study for years at expensive universities to become familiar with the myriad of regulations that tell us what is right and what is wrong. You end up with the rich getting away with doing the wrong thing simply because they can buy teams of attorneys to steer them through all of the loopholes. Conversely, those of limited means are left open to have their lives disrupted and destroyed by vindictive, power-crazed cops and prosecutors when they do little or nothing wrong. The legislative branch of government has evidently managed to arrange a system that defeats its very purpose.

When you look at the volume of money poured into the legislative system in terms of: a) salaries and expenses for the politicians and their staff, b) election campaign contributions used to buy legislators, and c) lobbying efforts used to bribe and influence the politicians, you are looking at quite a considerable chunk of money being filtered out of our collective pockets.

National Defense

Almost all industrialized nations of the world today employ standing military forces for the spurious purpose of "national defense." The influences and interests behind professional militaries have no interest or concern with defense. Militaries are all about creating excuses to spend tax revenue. They are not formed to protect the citizens of a nation, they exist to engage in profitable wars which both funnel money into corrupt hands and preoccupy masses with dangerous circumstances, distracting them from their leaders' covert criminal activity.

Standing armies are extremely expensive to maintain. This fact alone makes their existence a primary attraction for our plutocratic lords. The public is burdened with the continual cost of supporting the basic administration and running costs of the military. Compound this with the amount of taxpayer dollars fed to defense contractors to supply the military with their weapons (an astronomical amount when large-scale conflicts are underway) and you have an enormous drain on any economy — a drain that could be plugged up and return great amounts of wealth back into workers' pockets.

Those that tell us that we need standing forces at the ready for our protection are either naive enough to think that the profiteers of war will not stoop to creating the threats of war, or are themselves profiting from war.

Citizenship & Immigration

Citizenship is not an issue which has considerable direct influence upon the economy. It is, however, an important issue from a cultural standpoint and this has indirect but far-reaching effects on the economy and the overall health of the society.

Citizenship is traditionally bestowed upon anyone who is born in a particular location. It can also be attained by those who qualify and are willing to navigate the bureaucratic red tape that is often involved. This implies acceptance into a society with all of its attendant benefits based simply upon where one is located geographically.

While this has historically been a matter of practicality due to the unavailability of rapid transit, it is becoming irrelevant in modern times. One can make one's way to any corner of the Earth one desires relatively easily. So to base acceptance into a society upon geographical location is rapidly losing practicality. Citizenship and social rights should be attained through contribution to society. In today's outdated systems, they are granted primarily on the basis of where you were born and where you reside.

It is like choosing a spouse based solely on their relative proximity to you. Once upon a time, spouses were chosen this way out of necessity; especially in rural areas during times when horseback was the fastest means of transportation. However, times have changed. Today, people choose their spouse for personal reasons with little regard for where they live; it has become quite common to choose a spouse from foreign lands.

And so out of this rises the confusion of immigration. Governments have taken it upon themselves to determine where people have the right to live based on little more than arbitrary dictates. Regardless of how productive and valuable a person may be, he is not a citizen with full rights and conveniences if he was born in another part of the world.

In the United States strict, arbitrary qualifications are placed on immigration based, in part, on the misguided notion that immigrants will take locals' jobs. It is a concern born out of an inability of our governments to manage economies. More people will result in more productivity and more consumption as long as the general economic infrastructure and management is sound. It is just as much an opportunity for local companies to expand their businesses as there is the threat of job loss — provided you have a well-managed, viably functioning economy. A well-managed economy can only gain strength from increased numbers, provided those numbers consist of genuine individuals. Those that aren't genuine can be quickly weeded out with effective justice.

If people immigrating are in any way hostile, then they are actually invading and need to be dealt with accordingly. If immigrants are keen to contribute to the society they are joining, then it is simply a matter of good economic and social management to make it work. But *contribute* is a key word here. That means adding to what exists—adopting local ways and being productive. Immigrants that resist adopting local languages, customs and manners are not contributing, they are trying to impose their own way of life—trying to supplant what exists with what they bring. That is an invasion. It is not violent, but it is an invasion nonetheless. Just as it is very bad manners to enter another's home and not respect their ways, immigrating and refusing to adopt local conventions will naturally breed resentment.

One point well worth considering: If an inordinate number of people are moving from one place to another, it would be wise to honestly ask, "What circumstances are driving such a migration?" An honest answer will reveal a great deal.

THE SOLUTION: VIABLE STATECRAFT

Meritocratic Elections

To the degree that an alternative currency like Exchange Time comes into use, the existing governmental institutions will lose their revenue and fail. For this reason, any purpose to bring financial and economic reform must include attention to practical management of the public affairs which will be supported by and vitally reliant upon the currency and its related economic machinery.

The first question to address in the management of those public affairs is how to appoint leaders; how to decide who sits in that critical seat of responsibility for an entire community.

It is common belief that power corrupts. It is understandable to think such, but it is a fallacy. Power itself does not corrupt. It often seems so simply because the corrupt swarm into positions of power and will employ all manner of criminal devices to get there. Those of sound mind and honest intent do not normally pursue such positions with the same ferocious, psychotic obsession and, sadly, often decline to subject themselves to the company of the type of people they find in these circles. Most benevolent people would not be corrupted by power if they found themselves in high office. They might be corrupted by covert influences and sinister elements, but would fail in judgment or through lack of good information. Power does not breed megalomania any more than trees breed birds. One may look at a tree, find a bird there and without looking any deeper, offhandedly decide that trees must cause birds to come into existence. But that, too, would be a fallacy.

However, because the evil and the corrupt often do crave positions of power, the appointment of leaders is a crucial issue and has rightly been a topic of hot debate throughout history. The ancient Greeks and the Founding Fathers of the United States made huge advances in the subject without whom we would likely all be hopeless subjects of some overt, warmongering dictator or monarch, as so many in history before us have. It simply will not do to allow some individual the autocratic right to do as they please and appoint whomever they choose to whichever post they see fit.

Neither will it do to have some democracy pretending to grant power to the people so that the controllers of the modern propaganda machines can sway opinions, and hence, appoint leaders as they choose. There was no television or radio in ancient Greece or in colonial America. Democratic institutions were relatively sound solutions in those times. They are no longer. The opinions of too many are now in the hands of the plutocrats who control the information that naturally steers opinion.

People need a more direct, more immediate option available to them for enacting their will concerning the people that hold sway over important matters in their life. If you give people the option of cancelling their membership—of halting their patronage and participation altogether at any time they choose, the officials making important decisions will have a much greater incentive to make positively sure they don't screw around. How can you call a people free that have to wait for elections to come around, have to hope that others don't vote for the corrupt and stupid, and have to just live with it if deplorable fools do get into office by some apparently democratic method?

Even if people are given an option for withdrawing from some social leadership or another, one must have a sound system for the appointment of those carrying public responsibility. It is too important a matter to leave to arbitrary whim and opinion.

How should those in public office be appointed? Leaders and people of responsibility must be appointed according to results and ability alone. Not hype, not slogans, not catchy graphics and stirring music in a 30 second television commercial. Results and the ability to achieve results that benefit the society at large must form the totality of the criteria that appoints our leaders. The inane drivel and superficial pomp that constitute modern politicians' "platforms" is downright appalling. We should have the most brilliant minds, the cream of genius analysts and elite managing wizards in our positions of public office. Instead, we have a prevalence of political actors that possess questionable intellect and often seem hard-pressed to read their speeches without making fools of themselves. We must enact a system that filters out the inept and corrupt from places of power.

A meritocracy uses ability and merit as the criteria for the appointment of authority, rather than popularity which is the criteria used in democratic elections.

Under a system that accomplishes such, the people can be confident that capable and effective leaders are in control and that the corrupt will be unable to maintain positions of responsibility. Using such a system, society will flourish with competent direction and management, and the people can go about building prosperous lives unfettered by criminal warmongers, undistracted by blabbering politicians continually vying for our attention.

In order to do this, we first need to establish exactly what the proper product is for each executive social administrator in the society. A system that tracks the productivity of each executive administrator and appoints according to a track record of productivity is crucial. It is essential that it be comprehensive and fair, and must function according to measurable, verifiable results that do not require significant human opinion or evaluation. Figure out what a public official is supposed to produce, measure what they produce and promote or demote according to those criteria.

Instead of democratic elections, meritocratic elections consisting of periodical production reports will determine whether an official retains office, is demoted or is removed from office altogether. The wider the scope of responsibility, the longer it takes for executive measures to show broad effect. Therefore, the higher the rank of official, the longer the period should be between production reports—the longer the term in office.

While such a system will improve the quality of leadership in society, no system is perfect, and all systems are prone to being corrupted by the selfish and the foolish. Therefore, Social Viability retains the right to cancel the membership of any person or business that violates the policies of Social Viability. This is the safety valve that prevents any one official from wreaking havoc from a position of power. And, as always, any member of Social Viability retains the right to cancel their membership and organize their social activity otherwise at any time.

It is your choice. You can either have your leaders determined by a superficial popularity contest or you can have your leaders appointed according to their competence. A person whose job depends upon popularity will be good at smiling, shaking hands and telling people what they want to hear. A person whose job depends on being good at their assigned job will be good at their assigned job.

Direct Service-Based Payment

Social Viability's social management policy does not include any income tax paid to any government. There is no collection of taxed revenue at all by public institutions.

Enterprises that provide public services bill those public that use the services rendered. Novel idea, no? Itemized statements are rendered and bills are paid. If bills aren't paid, the people who fail to pay are denied nonessential services. Bills for essential services that aren't paid are tallied into emergency loans in the recipient's name.

One Law

Benevolent and civilized people do not need extensive systems of laws. The vast majority of people simply wish to be given the opportunity to build their lives within a fair and equitable social framework.

Those that constitute a minority that will cheat, steal and swindle for personal gain can be kept in check with simple and firm justice that is guided by a single timeless law: The law of right and wrong. From a social standpoint, right denotes those actions which support or contribute to the well-being of the community and those that live in it. Wrong denotes those actions which detract from or damage the well-being of the community and those that live in it.

Right and wrong must be judged on a case by case basis. To pass blanket legislation that explains in detail what acts are right and wrong is impractical, if not childish. Social policy delineates the agreements and procedures concerning social interaction and transaction, but there need not be laws saying that it is wrong to do bad things. An act that is wrong in one case may be wholly justified in another. Shooting a man in order to rob him is wrong (and the criminal doesn't need laws saying that murder and robbery are wrong to tell him that). Shooting a violent intruder threatening your family is wholly justified.

If accusations are brought against a person, he is brought before a panel of citizens that is similar to a jury. First it is determined whether or not the accused actually carried out the action (or failed to carry out a needed action) as charged. The facts must contain only physical evidence and firsthand testimony and must convincingly demonstrate commission (or failure to act) if the point is contested by the accused.

Then the panel of citizens must determine if the action was wrong. It is important that the evidence does not include how one or another person *feels* about what happened. People's feelings are volatile and subject to all manner of influence that are not necessarily relevant to the matter of whether an act was right or wrong. The act must be determined to be right or wrong according to the actual, hard results that unfolded.

Mitigating circumstances must not be ignored in the evaluation of the act. For example, if a person stole a car in order to get emergency treatment for a seriously injured person, the mitigating circumstances must be taken into account.

Also, if a man challenges another to a one-on-one fist fight and is beaten, the man dealing out the beating cannot be charged provided the fight was not taken beyond its reasonable end with the use of excessive, vicious malice—for instance, kicking an unconscious man repeatedly about the head. If an aggressor challenges another who declines to fight, but the aggressor then attacks anyway, the aggressor should be brought to justice for obvious reasons. The point is that people should be held to account for what they get themselves into and should not use social justice as a get-even. Justice is used to contain violence and dishonest conduct against unwilling victims. It has nothing to do with willing participants engaged in dangerous activities of their own free—and sometimes foolish—choice.

If the accused is found guilty of an act and that act is found to be damaging to an unwilling victim or their property, the panel assesses the extent of damage caused. If a car was stolen and wrecked, the damage would equal the value of the car, the extra costs (of a rental car, for example) incurred by the person whose car was stolen, the cost of the investigations to prove the perpetrator's guilt, and the cost of the justice proceedings. The individual would then be sentenced to pay a fine equaling twice that of the total damage caused. Additionally, they would have their citizenship rank reduced to a degree that is commensurate with the offense as determined by the panel of citizens.

If the guilty party refuses to cooperate or to pay the fine or to repent, his Social Viability membership is revoked and he is relegated to the status of foreign individual. As such, he can no longer hold a trade account and use the Exchange Time currency. As a foreign individual he should be imprisoned if he is guilty of an act that brought physical harm to a person.

It is not a complicated issue and needs neither a complicated system of laws nor any conceited legislative body to define them for us.

Aside from criminal matters, there is a moral obligation to mind your manners. This is important. People should be held accountable for actions that, while not causing actual harm to person or property, cause others distress and discomfort. Many people would find it quite offensive to see another running naked down the street. It does actual harm to no one, but it can be offensive. Moral codes should be assembled by societies, voted upon, and observed. It need only deal with manners and provide a basis of how people should interact so as to get along amicably. It need not apply to any act that incurs damage that will require people's time and expense to repair or set right. That is covered by the law of right and wrong and is dealt with accordingly. Those found guilty of these moral—rather than criminal—transgressions should be subjected to penalties that involve loss of citizenship rank and privilege rather than by fines, loss of membership and imprisonment as covered above.

Self-Defense

The best way to demonstrate that contemporary professional "defense forces" are merely profiteering mechanisms is to juxtapose them with more ideal notions. If we start from scratch and address the subject of most effectively defending one's land from aggressive invasion we will see how an ideal scene would depart from the existing facade.

There are several points that must preface this subject which are senior to the issue and cannot be ignored in dealing with this matter. First, the most powerful ingredient in defense is a prosperous, highly productive economy. Having the strength of production to support such a large effort as warfare is essential. Second, a society must be honest with itself in treating other groups and societies with respect and integrity. Exploiting others is never excusable. It is a sign of weakness and greed. It degrades everyone involved and provokes violence. Third, diplomacy and reason should be used to their full extent to prevent aggression. Warfare is the manifestation of a social degeneration into a mob psychosis and should be prevented at all reasonable costs. However, that cost must never include enslavement or a concession to a situation that will lead to such.

Having said that, in preparation for such extreme events as a hostile invasion there are things that should be done—and preparations should always be taken to provide for all manner of possible disasters.

First, arm your populace. Ask any general and he will tell you that the most difficult force to take over is a guerilla force on its own turf. The USSR couldn't subdue Afghanistan and the mighty United States could not win in Vietnam. When your supplies are right at hand, when you are familiar with the terrain and the resources available, when you are hard to find and spread throughout an area, when you are difficult to identify, the deck is stacked heavily in your favor. An invading army must travel to fight on your ground and this exponentially increases the cost of the fight for them in relation to the distance they must travel.

Second, train your entire populace in combat and survival. Make your people tough and ready. Reward people for being valuable defense assets to your society. All of the men, if not all of the men *and* women, should be trained in hand to hand combat, basic weapons combat, weapons construction and maintenance, tactics, survival, reconnaissance and intelligence. If successful in this endeavor, any aggressor would face an impossible task of invasion and conquest.

Lastly, ensure that your populace never makes a full-time occupation out of warfare or the preparation thereof. Defense preparations must always consist of contingency plans and not become primary concerns unless war breaks out. Thus, your populace remains productive in building the prosperity that is needed in the event that conflict erupts. Also, your populace will remain primarily focused on the positive and constructive effort of building strength and vitality in their society as opposed to becoming so involved and immersed in warfare and combat as to develop a sordid thirst for it—a most unfortunate scenario.

If, in the most extreme case, a hostile force seeks to use air forces or artillery to utterly destroy rather than merely conquer your land and people, you must have evacuation plans in place. When confronted with such a degree of diabolical insanity, all manner of covert operations should be employed to sabotage such efforts. However, to stoop to the same level by constructing the same weapons and using them in the commission of similarly horrendous crimes leads nowhere but to the same despicable state that you seek to defeat. If one becomes evil in order to combat evil, is evil ever really defeated? Mass destruction of human life is nowhere on the path of improvement and advancement for mankind. Defense is defense. Weapons designed to decimate and obliterate on a large scale do not fall into this category.

With such a manner of self-defense, the entire population can remain in a healthy state of productivity whilst remaining essentially unconquerable.

Modern so-called "defense forces" not only suck colossal wealth from nations' budgets, they create entire economic sectors that come to depend on the outbreak of war to make their profits. This scenario must never be tolerated. If man is to ever really become civilized, we must dissolve the vested interests that provoke and incite war for profit.

Immigrant Relations

Because Social Viability is built around the productivity of a society, rather than around a geographical location, the matter of which people live in a given location is an entirely different issue.

With Social Viability, members of the same society can be living in entirely different parts of the world. They are linked by the production of goods and services that can be sold to people in other societies.

Members of Social Viability have no reason to contend the issue of who lives where so long as those that move into an area do not tread on the toes of those already there. If immigrants to an area are destructive, counterproductive or intrusive, they must be treated as a hostile invasion and with a severity of response that is commensurate with the threat posed.

The methods of dealing with them may range from trade sanctions through to the use of force. Again, the manner of dealing with intruders must be consistent with the threat they pose. Littering immigrants should not be shot, but neither should an armed aggressor be merely placed under trade sanctions.

If immigrants to an area are not a threat or intrusion in any way—if they are found to be migrating for good reason and mean to be helpful, constructive and productive, trade with them, and even welcome them into your society if there's a mutual benefit to be had.

CHAPTER 4
SOCIAL DIGNITY

THE PROBLEM: LEGAL SYSTEM

The Product of an Attorney

A N ATTORNEY'S product is a case won in court or a favorable out-of-court settlement. This is what their occupational objectives are centered around. This is what brings home the bacon for them. Their objective is not to see that fair justice is done. It should be little wonder, then, that it is common to see injustices in the justice system.

It is supposedly the judge's job to see that justice is done. However, problems inevitably arise if the judge and an attorney on a case frequent the same country club. And since judges rise from the ranks of attorneys, it is a little absurd to think that judges are totally impartial when judging matters contested by their former peers. Ponder for a moment upon what it is that the most highly paid defense attorneys really offer their clients. Is it really their ability to argue a case that makes them worth millions to a rich defendant? Or is it their connections and relationships with judges and other authorities within the judicial system that make their services so valuable?

What about the jury? They don't have any vested interests in the outcomes of trials. This is true and is what makes them a valid component of the justice system. If only the attorneys weren't allowed to manipulate those that constitute the jury. Having an influence on what jurors make up a jury in a trial is a crucial aspect to a case and the attorneys know it. When a defense attorney's lavish income is determined by whether he wins or loses cases, do you think he is going to leave crucial matters to chance?

Additionally, judges arbitrarily influence what is brought before a jury in court of law. Determining what the jury sees in court naturally has a crucial bearing on the verdict reached. So, while the jury may be somewhat impartial, they have little power to see justice properly done.

When well-financed vested interests enter into the justice system, impartiality goes out the window, and right along with it, fair delivery of justice codes. Rich men get away with murder because they have the money to buy expensive, influential teams of lawyers. Poor men go to jail for minor or even no crime at all because they can't afford to defend themselves. This is not justice. This is oppression of the poor and unfortunate.

Justice can only work if it functions impartially and equally for all strata of society. Society cannot function in a healthy and productive fashion if it does not have a justice system that actually carries out justice.

There is a great deal of money made out of the legal system; money that could contribute to the prosperity of the economy; money that attracts corruption like a flame attracts moths. The amount of money that is spent manipulating justice can be seen in the prevalent and lavish law offices in every big city in the west. This considerable amount of money is being misspent and Lady Justice is being prostituted in the process.

Courts Promoting Criminality

Courts throughout the United States—and undoubtedly around the world—make a great deal of money simply because crimes occur. The fees and court costs charged to process the arrests and hearings of relatively petty crime are quite significant. Crime pays alright—just not for the criminals.

When the government launches campaigns to fight drugs or stop drunk-driving or whatever is in vogue, it is not out of genuine concern for the public. Government entities have demonstrated that they couldn't care less about the safety, welfare, and prosperity of the people at large. No, their crime fighting campaigns and crackdowns are plainly designed to feed people through the justice system and to generate plenty of revenue from traffic and parking violations. The courts make money when a man is arrested. It is therefore in the interests of the government to have people arrested—a very dangerous situation indeed. You will find that known repeat offenders will be given swift treatment through the court systems so that they can be released back onto the streets to be picked up again and so keep the cycle going. There is no incentive to actually reduce crime. If crime does decline, people will begin to be arrested for lesser wrongs so as to maintain revenue. It is inevitable. It is a systemic corruption that is ignored by all but those that fall victim to it.

The money that pours through the court systems could be invested in productive works that actually contribute to the wealth of the society and its citizens, rather than promoting onerous and oppressive justice that most often targets those that suffer the most from lack of wealth.

Civil Suits Promoting Irresponsibility

Where you find people awarded large sums of money for plain clumsiness or for "not knowing" that something was bad for them, you find people that do not take responsibility for what happens to them. Where you find people unwilling to be responsible, you find people unable to create their own lot in life, unable to found an enterprise, unable to care for their family, unable to keep their own car from crashing into others' and unable to maintain a healthy and productive frame of mind. In other words, you get ever-worsening decadence. You find accidents being promoted with billboards advertising the fact that if you slip and fall you could be awarded money. The failure in logic that breeds paying people for having accidents is quite dangerous.

Civil suits are, by their very nature, invalid. If a suit has serious merit to it, it needs to be heard as a criminal matter. Otherwise, the plaintiffs and the money-grubbing lawyers that promote the entire sordid affair would be well encouraged to discover that a person can in fact be responsible for their own lives and what happens to them.

Furthermore, the economy suffers from the situation. The money sponged up in civil courts could be going into the creation of a society that the citizens could be proud of and, more importantly, be responsible for.

Law Enforcement: The Criminal's Dream

A person with violent criminal tendencies would look at the occupation of police officer and drool. To be given a firearm, a car and permission to beat the heck out of people and even shoot at them if provided the slightest provocation would be a criminal's dream.

Of course if a criminal's career has begun before it occurs to him to join the force, then his record will prevent him from getting his crisp new uniform, expensive gun, and personal vehicle. However, this is little more than an issue of demographics. In poorer urban areas, in minority cultures, overt criminal activity is more prevalent. The criminally inclined in these areas are much more likely to have run-ins with the law at a young age and so miss the opportunity to become a police officer.

In less poverty-stricken strata of society, gangs are not recruiting and the police are not patrolling so any criminal acts are less likely to lead to arrest. Therefore, in these demographics you find more opportunity to be the cop rather than the robber—the legal thug rather than the illegal one.

This is not to say that all cops are criminally inclined. This is to say that it is dangerous to make the profession of law enforcement attractive to criminals.

Furthermore, the entire practice of law enforcement is a fundamentally flawed notion. If anyone needs to be forced to do the right thing and refrain from felonious conduct, they have no place in a civilized society. Such a person must be rejected by society wholesale and treated as a foreign enemy. And if that small minority were treated as such society would be a very peaceful place. Unfortunately, it serves the ends of the puppet masters that own us to have criminals running around among us.

Police officers spend a lot of time doing very little. Despite the abundant fear mongering that you may consume through the news media, there just isn't that much crime to attend to. Take away the policing of traffic offenses and attending traffic accidents and the police have very little left to do—unless of course there is a public demonstration of some government measure underway. Then you will see cops out in full riot gear to enforce obedience.

Law enforcement is too well funded, plain and simple. Giving the governments armies of thugs to enforce their will is a dire mistake and yet another significant drain on the resources of the economy.

The Prison Industry

Possibly the greatest tragedy of the malfunctioning legal system is the prisons. They are an industry all unto themselves in the United States today and there is very little said about it for good—or, more accurately, bad—reason.

While politicians regurgitate mindless slogans for democracy and its freedoms, droves of people are being locked away for nonviolent crimes in the United States. Why? Prisons are run by corporations that are paid by the various governments for the service of imprisoning their criminals. These corporations know that there is an obscene amount of money up for grabs so they buy up politicians who institute hard-line sentencing policies. Of course the official line is, "tougher sentencing so as to reduce crime." Sounds great to the casual observer who takes no further notice. So the prisons fill up and the corporate interests erect more prisons for their political pawns to fill up once more.

There is a great deal of money swindled out of the peoples' economy by the prison industry. It is money that is being conned out of every honest man and woman. However, that crime pales in comparison to the human rights atrocity that is unjustly imprisoning people for monetary profit.

People's lives are all but ripped from them when they are thrown in jail. There is no rebuilding one's life whilst locked in a cage. In a civilized society it must be a measure of last resort to imprison a person—done simply to protect the life and limb of productive people in society. In fact, a culture that uses prison as a punishment—let alone as a means to make money—rather than simple protection of the public is not worthy of the term civilized. It is debased and when capital punishment is added into the equation, it is downright twisted. No matter how you slice it, executing criminals is an act of revenge, emotionally driven, having very little productive basis in reason.

We are not civilized because our politicians wear suits and meet in ornate buildings. We are not free because we have a wide range of TV channels to choose from when we watch the news and listen to our politicians try to convince us we are free.

Civilization is marked by the advancement of technology; by understanding; by harmonious, rational behavior; by organized, effective social activity; and by sublime creativity. Freedom is marked by the absence of onerous burdens employed by corrupt parasites that feed on the productivity of others. I see a great deal of room for improvement.

THE SOLUTION: VIABLE JURISPRUDENCE

Responsibility

One of the most important things that a society can foster in its constituents is responsibility; responsibility for one's own actions; responsibility for one's family; responsibility for what happens in one's place of work; responsibility for what happens in one's society.

Justice simply cannot be carried out with any degree of effectiveness if a high level of responsibility is not present in those administering the justice. Justice is the reigning in of those that do not, by their own determination, act in a fair and benevolent manner in their actions. In order to enact justice, responsibility for the actions of the perpetrator and the repercussions of the crime must be taken. One who isn't fully willing to right the wrongs committed by others will not carry out justice but will enact revenge in a hateful, resentful and destructive manner. Vengeance is not justice. It is using the crime of another to justify one's own crime.

No aspect of a justice system should substitute or discourage responsibility in any way—it is the foundation upon which justice can exist.

Self-Representation

Self-representation is a vital part of responsible justice. Those who prefer to hide behind a lawyer rather than stand up and answer for their actions are exactly the people who wish not to take responsibility for what they do. Of course, a legal system that has become so complex as to require a lawyer to navigate its proceedings is entirely dysfunctional to begin with, and is often rendered null and void before the first piece of evidence on a case is heard. If a man is forced to hire a lawyer just to know how to argue a case in a court of law, then the purpose of justice is well and truly defunct.

If a court case is limited to an honest, reasonable hearing of the evidence at hand based upon the case in and of itself, independent of what may or may not have happened in the past to set "legal precedence," then there is no reason a person would need legal representation. To use legal precedence in the demonstration of some rightness or wrongness is to assume that all circumstances and repercussions are the same in both cases. Such an inane practice is a direct result of not wishing to take responsibility for confronting and evaluating a given case on its own merits and has no place in determining a person's guilt or innocence. Justice must be consistent and fair, but legal precedence brings more convoluted subterfuge and robotic detachment to the courtroom than it is worth.

Those who are genuinely unable to speak for themselves due to some physical or mental condition have no place in a justice system and need to have a guardian appointed to take responsibility for them and their actions.

Judicial Hearings

When a charge of wrong-doing is brought against someone, they are notified immediately and presented with copies of all evidence being filed against them. A date is set for the hearing that is as soon as possible. If the defendant requests additional time to acquire evidence, it is granted under reasonable conditions and the filer of the charges is immediately notified of the request.

At the hearing, the only people present are an administrator to run the hearing (along with any assistants they may need), the defendant, and a jury of no less than five and no more than ten. The evidence that was filed against the defendant is brought before the court, including any witnesses. Following that, the defendant is given the opportunity to defend themselves by attempting to demonstrate that either they did not commit the act/s in question or that the act/s were justified under the circumstances and were not, in fact, wrong. They may present any evidence that is relevant, including witness testimony. After all evidence has been presented, the jury votes. No deliberation is made among jurors. Any juror may be given one full day to consider before casting their vote, but no more.

If the vote is split equally or in favor of the defendant, they are acquitted and the filer of charges is charged the cost of the court hearing. If the filer of charges so requests, the costs may be deferred to a second hearing pending a new presentation of the evidence.

If the vote of more than half of the jury is that the defendant was guilty of committing a harmful crime against an unwilling victim, the defendant is to pay the equivalent of twice the damage caused in the crime, twice the cost of the court hearings, and twice the cost of any and all investigations that were used to gather evidence against them.

If someone is guilty of a crime that brought intentional or reckless physical harm such as murder, rape, unprovoked assault, manslaughter, etc., then they are to have their membership to the society suspended immediately, be isolated from society in a prison and have offered to them rehabilitation services that, upon completion of which, will restore their full membership and freedom to live among others in society. Note that if rehabilitation is accepted by the guilty, membership is not entirely revoked; it is merely suspended. If rehabilitation is refused or not honestly undertaken, then membership is revoked altogether and they are kept imprisoned until such time as they agree to rehabilitation programs.

Revoked membership may be reinstated if special application is made at a later time, but very strong evidence of worthiness needs to be presented in such a case. The criteria for those to regain membership after it has been fully revoked must be necessarily much more stringent than those who cooperate and have a suspended membership restored.

If someone is found guilty of a nonviolent crime such as fraud or theft that did not involve intentional or reckless physical harm, then the fine will suffice. No imprisonment is necessary. Any flat refusal or failure to pay the fine will result in suspended membership. Failure to pay would be defined as not making sufficient regular payments that demonstrate an honest intention to pay off the fine. Rehabilitation should be offered along with suspension and should be followed by full revocation if not honestly undertaken. Again, imprisonment is not necessary unless intentional or reckless physical harm is perpetrated.

If property is criminally stolen or damaged, it is to be replaced or repaired with an emergency loan as soon as the perpetrator is found guilty in a properly conducted court case. That loan is repaid by the social judiciary fund. The emergency loan is repaid immediately if there is sufficient money available in that fund. If there is not sufficient money available, it stays on the social account as an outstanding debt until such time as there is enough in the social judiciary fund to pay. The social judiciary fund is made up of the fines paid by convicted criminals. Guilty criminals pay a fine equal to double the damage caused and so the social judiciary fund should not run dry, even accounting for those criminals that take their unpaid fines to the grave.

If the cost in a crime is human life as opposed to mere property, repayment of the fine can only be made by the restoration of another person to membership. Rehabilitation of another imprisoned criminal after having completed one's own rehabilitation would amount to this. This would entail considerable application in criminal rehabilitation activities without pay or exchange for their time. When a dangerous criminal is rehabilitated single-handedly—or a number of dangerous criminals when a part of a like-numbered team—it can be said that they have repaid their debt of one human life.

If a defendant or filer of charges believes that a wrong decision has been reached in court, appeals may be made, but no more than three times by either party. As such, a hearing will be heard a maximum of six times in the unlikely event that both defendant and filer of charges appeal three times each. Where at all possible, the original jurors are retained for each appeal hearing so as to save time familiarizing new jurors with the case.

When appeals are made, the costs of all hearings added together will constitute the court costs that must be paid.

The aim is to have charges brought only when the issue can be conclusively proven and for appeals to occur only when the appellant is confident that their case has not been heard accurately and that another presentation of their evidence (or new evidence) will sway the decision. Knowing that one will have to pay the costs for further hearings will dissuade people from appealing if they do not have valid and compelling evidence to present.

Defendants may hire investigators to help them acquire evidence, but must always appear in person and speak for themselves at the hearing. Accusers may hire investigators to accumulate evidence against someone that they want brought to justice but no one may ever hire an investigator and remain undisclosed as an accuser.

This court system is designed to address wrongdoings with a minimum of fuss and red tape in an honest, effective and straightforward manner. People must be held responsible for the accusations they bring against others and this arrangement makes it such. Covert elements seeking to bring charges against persons are strictly forbidden and must be prevented.

Membership Responsibility

The profession of law enforcement as we know it today has no place in Social Viability's justice systems. First of all, having armed police "to protect us" has the subtle effect of turning people into cowards. In the absence of police, people learn how to defend themselves and learn to confront, monitor and take responsibility for their surroundings. Without police, a culture of personal responsibility can grow in which bystanders intervene in crimes as they occur.

If thugs band together and threaten the peace, a defense force should be called together. Organization needs to be in place to rapidly call together such forces when they are needed. Any person or group, within or without, that becomes overtly violent and demonstrates an inability to be a part of civilized society, needs to be treated as a foreign entity. Dangerous foreign entities are to be handled as swiftly as possible by defense forces consisting of able-bodied—and preferably well-trained—citizens.

It must be reiterated that the simple fact of living in a common area does not grant common inclusion in civilized society. Membership is granted readily, but it is maintained and ranked through benevolence and contribution. Overt, intended physical harm toward members of the society incurs immediate suspension of membership which will be revoked altogether if rehabilitation efforts are not readily cooperated with. Such is the only basis whereby relative strangers can trust one another and live in productive harmony.

Where crimes are committed, it is the job of any and every member of society to do something about it. If someone sells you a product fraudulently, you should report them and charge them with the crime committed. They will have their hearing and be dealt with accordingly.

If someone steals your car and you have no idea who perpetrated the crime, you may hire an investigator to track down the criminal who did it and, if sufficient evidence is uncovered, you can report and charge.

If someone commits a crime against you and you can't prove that they did, then you better make sure that if it happens again, you can. Remember, emergency loans for stolen goods are granted only if the perpetrator is found guilty in a properly conducted court case. If someone does you wrong, prove it and those crimes committed against you will be redressed.

If someone is charged and refuses to appear for their hearing, they are found guilty of the crime charged and if they do not come forward and pay their dues, they will have their social membership revoked.

Professional investigators may earn a living as hired hands, helping those that have been cheated, robbed or wronged in some way. They may also patrol and use surveillance to uncover criminal activity and charge the perpetrators themselves. They will be paid for their time in due course if they are competent, but they act as independent, private professionals, not uniformed government police. This is a vital distinction to make. Police officers, sheriffs and law enforcement agents carry out a governmental function and are paid to make sure people remain obedient, governed subjects and follow the laws that control their lives and behavior. Private investigators work for the people that hire them or, in the end, work for the criminal in bringing them to justice—for when the guilty is fined, the investigator is paid. And this is as it should be: the investigator is doing the criminal a great service by bringing them to justice. The life of a criminal is one of degradation and fear. Applying good justice, halting a person's path down a depraved criminal path is not only of great service to the society at large, it is of great service to the criminal themselves.

People can live in harmony and take responsibility for their societies. All they need is the chance to do so.

Criminal Rehabilitation

In a society that is focused on productivity and creativity, endeavors must be made to turn all problematic and unfavorable situations into positive ones. There are no more important examples of this than in criminal rehabilitation. It is very possible to turn the vast majority of criminals around and have them lead productive lives on their own determinism. The main reason that criminal rehabilitation does not widely occur in the prison industry is that rehabilitation is not in the interests of the industry itself. Criminals who become yet more hardened in the degrading prisons in which they do time are far more likely to return to jail after release and garner more profits for the slave-owners.

Criminals imprisoned should not be given set terms of imprisonment. Sentencing as we know it is a reflection of the punishment and revenge mentality, as opposed to rehabilitation-oriented systems. With Social Viability, if someone is imprisoned, they serve until they demonstrate conclusively that they can be productive members of society. If they fake it, manage to fool those administering the system and later return to jail, they will face much tougher release criteria.

It is important to remember that the proportion of truly wicked individuals is not very high. Many violent criminals will be readily rehabilitated when given the chance. A long-term inmate would be one that has been in prison for more than five years—those that refuse to cooperate and rehabilitate. Other than those that need to be taught to read from scratch, for example, there are few that would need to be kept inside for longer than five years when an effective and honest rehabilitation program is used fully. Those long-term criminals that resist rehabilitation are not necessarily the direct perpetrators of overt, violent crime. They are often easily overlooked accomplices—usually more sinister than the actual perpetrator; the type of psychotic criminal that will gleefully warp others and encourage them to commit violent crime. These are the particularly dangerous individuals that are guilty of more covert crimes of a sicker nature. They are harder to apprehend because they perpetrate their wickedness behind closed doors, with whispers and suggestions, but they are far more important to be isolated from society because these are the ultimate sources of social ills. Where you find people going crazy and becoming violent, you will find one of society's most dangerous criminals in the background urging it all on.

Lastly, but not at all least importantly, is the issue of how to treat prisoners. They must be treated with humanity. No criminal is ever rehabilitated when treated with scorn and disgust. Successful efforts to rehabilitate should be carried out with respect and dignity. The criminal that is truly confronting his sins and climbing out of the pit of self-degradation that is the criminal state is engaging in a very courageous task. Those that insist on being evil and wicked should be as isolated as possible, especially from other inmates. Give them as little as possible to hurt while still providing humane and stimulating facilities.

A society that is troubled by few criminals living among its populace will be successful. A society that routinely turns criminals into worthy citizens will be truly magnificent.

CHAPTER 5
DISCRETION IN BUSINESS

THE PROBLEM: CORRUPTED INDUSTRIES

Pharmaceutical Industry & Medical Field

A LARGE proportion of the medical field and almost the entire pharmaceutical industry are, together, downright psychotic in nature. If a man destroys himself with crazy obsessions that are blatantly destructive, despite the ready availability of practical solutions to his problems and, at the same time, asserts that he is doing well and solving his problems, one would reasonably determine that he is psychotically dangerous to himself, and potentially to others as well. So too, when a sector of society does these things, it must be deduced that that sector of society is, for all intents and purposes, psychotic.

When dangerous and destructive drugs and treatments are used on a routine basis to solve elementary problems, all under the guise of medical therapy, one can't help but shake one's head in wonder at times.

A most glaringly vile example is the widespread psychiatric drugging of children with "behavioral problems," let alone the adult population. Children, lacking exercise and being fed atrocious diets of processed foods with copious sugar intake that become tired, restless, and agitated are diagnosed with "mental illnesses" and prescribed dangerous psychotropic drugs. The so-called "research studies" that supposedly prove that these drugs are necessary are used to convince insane notions to parents and schools that would prefer not to be responsible for their children and students. It truly is tragic and is a very disturbing indication of the level of decadence that has afflicted our culture. It never seems to occur to these parents and teachers that drug companies make billions of dollars annually from these destructive products and that, because of this, they will not hesitate to manufacture fraudulent "proof." The people taking care of our future generations would do well to start questioning the motives of the influences at work.

The gargantuan pharmaceutical industry has no justification for its existence beyond the production of a very few substances necessary to handle emergency medical situations.

Many medical professionals have become mere dealers for these drug companies, dolling out pills on a routine basis. Physicians spend so little time studying nutrition and so much time studying side effects of medications. It is patently evident that a person can lead a very healthy life, without the affliction of any of the major diseases assaulting our populations, all through good, additive-free nutritional intake—and, no, that doesn't mean drinking "diet" soda, consuming the instant TV dinners that merely have the word "healthy" on the package or eating cookies that contain "natural" flavors rather than "artificial" flavors. It means paying attention to your body, using sensible, non-destructive remedies, and fueling it with nutritious fuel, rather than addictive, destructive toxins.

Another deranged practice perpetrated by this sector of our society is mass inoculations with vaccines. Now I'm in no position to pass judgment on the validity of the basic theory of vaccination against disease, but I certainly have seen enough to know that the soup that they pump into our babies and children is toxic and dangerous. Make no mistake: there is big money to be made in making, distributing and issuing these shots laced with preservatives like mercury and formaldehyde. Fear mongering for profit has driven inoculation into the mainstream to the point where poisonous substances are being jabbed into people of all ages, including vulnerable infants, while a blind eye is turned to the autism and retardation it is causing. It would be laughable if it wasn't so sick. Again, it never seems to occur to many people to be suspicious of an industry that profits from the threat of disease outbreak. I wonder if people would be suspicious of a fox that announced that it should be hired to guard the chickens. I have never ever heard of any investigation or even mention of inquiry into the possibility of disease outbreaks being perpetrated by those with huge financial interests in their occurrence. The lack of investigation and inquiry is suspicious in and of itself, wouldn't you think?

The most crucial question to ask is: If the pharmaceutical and medical industries began prescribing treatments that actually made people healthy, how would they continue to make their billions? The answer: they couldn't. People would stop going to the doctor for the prescriptions.

Practical solutions take a back seat to profit-taking at the expense of the health and sanity of the general population in the upside-down approach to handling one of our primary assets: our physical bodies.

And as insignificant as it seems in comparison to the degeneration of our collective physical health, the economic impact of the billions being siphoned away in medical drugs and aberrant practices is nevertheless a significant issue in itself.

Arms Manufacturing

If an industry made enormous profits when wars were being fought and if the corporate interests comprising that industry also bought themselves great political influence in the developed countries of the world, would it really be any wonder that wars often break out around the world? The politicians' bosses—the banking and corporate wealth holders that fund the political process—make money when arms are used and destroyed. Wars don't just happen. They are incited and there is profit to be made from the pain and suffering. Today's influential leaders have blood dripping from their hands as they count their personal fortunes.

The world's governments manage our societies and set the course of events. When these governments purchase arms in massive quantities under the guise of "defense" you inevitably find yourself with militaristic states that will find all manner of excuse for killing someone or another. If they can't find someone to vilify, they will invent someone. There is too much money at stake to allow peace to exist.

Governments should not be purchasing massive quantities of weaponry on behalf of the people under the guise of protecting the people. The people should be encouraged to protect themselves and be free to each do so as they see fit. To do otherwise invites the widespread warmongering that is so common in today's world.

Modern Agriculture & Food Processing

For a so-called intelligent race to make and manufacture poison for food is preposterous. But when one judges our modern methods of feeding ourselves objectively, that is often what we do.

There are a few elementary things that need to be established in taking up this subject. It is absurd that these things need to be discussed, but in today's culture the subject is so far removed from simple logic that we do need to reexamine the subject virtually from scratch.

We eat the flesh and substance of living organisms because eating things rich in life maintains the life of our own living organism. We do not eat rock for lunch or sand for dinner. These things contain insufficient life. We sustain the life of our own biological organisms by feeding upon other living organisms.

So, having established that we need living matter to maintain the lives of our bodies, the question begs asking: Why do we process the life out of so much of the food we ingest? It is blatantly imbecile to cook, whip and process food products until they are unrecognizable substances, flavor and preserve them with all manner of poisonous chemical compounds, irradiate them, freeze them, cook them in a microwave and then chow the stuff down in front of the T.V.

So why do we do it? The short answer is money, laziness and shortsightedness. The corporations making our food can sell more at less cost when it has shelf-life, is cheap to make and is addictive. Dead, processed food lasts longer because it is very slow to rot. It is a matter of logistics. With our food sources so industrialized, massive plants supply food to vast areas. Also, the crud that is used for the ingredients of our food is inevitably cheaper to obtain than the real thing. And don't think that food producers wouldn't stop at deliberately making your food addictive so that they can count on your repeat business. Viable, healthy food production is just not practical for giant corporations whose sole focus is profit.

Livestock are kept in inhumane conditions, fed disgustingly poor quality food, and pumped full of hormones and antibiotics. Biotech corporations insist on genetically modifying organisms for the sole purpose of patenting them and monopolizing the food supply. Our food is a source of massive profit and that profit evidently sits much higher as a priority than our collective health and well-being.

Real Estate

When a person buys a piece of real estate, does little or nothing to upgrade or improve it, and then turns around to sell it at a profit within a relatively short period of time, the person has made money without providing any product or service—a corruption of the principles of money. It not so much a poor commentary on those that execute such deals as it is a vivid illustration of the folly of an economic system that rewards such commercial activity. Those that provide for their families and their future cannot be expected to restrain themselves from taking advantage of attractive capital gains in real estate deals. It is the commercial systems—the social framework—that must be corrected so as to promote viable commercial activity; commercial activity that will actually generate higher living standards for the society.

When a person owns a piece of real estate and charges rent to residents or businesses while retaining full ownership of that property, they are merely leeching upon the productivity of those leasing the property. A landowner that provides a place of residence or business is providing a very valuable product. But that does not change the fact that the lessee is, in essence, paying for the real estate when they pay rent, yet the title is never delivered to that person that pays for it.

Many a shrewd business person has purchased real estate and rented it so as to have the tenant pay the mortgage payments for them. Shrewd business people must be rewarded—and the commercial policies of Social Viability do just that. But the tenant that pays the mortgage should come into possession of that for which they have paid.

Anyone building and developing real estate; anyone repairing or upgrading property for a living; anyone leasing a property according to a fair lease-to-own arrangement is providing a useful service. These are the types of activities upon which the economy should ride.

Society as a whole, its prosperity, its stability, its cultural integrity gains when people become wealthy providing a worthwhile and positive service. It fails when people are allowed and encouraged to get rich in ways that provide no service or betterment to the society at large.

The amount of money absorbed into artificially inflating real estate markets and rental agreements could be forwarding the social prosperity and making those that do good works rich. Instead, it is funneling wealth away from productive people and granting it to those that have learned how to make money at others' expense.

High-Tech Industries

The problem with high-tech industries is not so much what is being done or how it is being done. The problem is primarily what's not being done. Technological advancement and capitalization on new developments are being stifled through misuse of the government patenting system.

If some independent person develops a new technology, it will very often threaten some existing multi-billion dollar industry. For example, if a person developed a propulsion device which rendered the internal-combustion engine obsolete, the entire motor vehicle industry is threatened, as is any other industry which is tied to it, like oil. Yes, these corporations could pick up the technology and attempt to lead the development and marketing of the new invention with the capital and wherewithal that they already posses, but they seem to see this as a risky venture compared with the existing, lucrative niche that is already carved out for them.

So, they are left with another technologically suppressing option. They can make an offer to the inventor to buy the patent. They can comfortably offer a sum which is a pittance to a multi-national corporation, but a fortune to an individual from the working class. Once the rights to a patent are owned, no one else is permitted by law to develop products using the invention.

They own it and can suppress the creation of potential competition by simply not developing the technology.

As such, the advancement and development of societies and cultures can be suppressed in the name of protecting private interests. The cost to society of such policy is virtually impossible to calculate. It is suffice to say that the cost to society of suppressing its development is the very future of the society itself.

THE SOLUTION: VIABLE SOCIAL POLICY

Nutritional Services & Competence Cultivation

A profession which deals with disease in, and damage to, human bodies independent of any other endeavor in society is dangerous. That business will inevitably develop an interest in people becoming sick and getting injured. We see this today. Powerful corporations that require disease to be widespread in order to maintain their profits are a clear danger.

The product of those attending to the health and well being of others must be: *Number of People Healthy*. This must constitute both the object and measure of performance so that the industry is working toward that product. If the entire profession is centered on the concept of having people get a nutritional intake and health care that will maintain genuine health and vitality, then human ingenuity will accomplish this. If the profession is centered on creating and patenting the most profitable medication for the alleviation of the symptoms of illness, then human ingenuity will not only make the medication, but make sure there are plenty of people who need it.

Obviously it must be a part of the function of those in nutritional services to attend to ill people and return them to sustained health as fast as possible. Every day that a person is unwell, the Number of People Healthy will be lower. However, the industry's entire incentive is to put the person back in good and lasting health. A person whose symptoms have merely abated will return to bad health unless the root cause of their condition has been properly addressed.

A related function must exist with the product of: *Number of People Uninjured*. They will be responsible for cultivating competence and eliminating unnecessarily dangerous hazards from society. They will be responsible for repairs to injured people including emergency surgery needed to keep people alive when afflicted with an injury.

Combat Self-Sufficiency

The people who purchase weapons must be the ones who are going to use them. This is because the buyers of weapons should be the ones who least want them to be used. The vast majority of people do not want to carry a weapon into mortal battle with other men. And of those that do want to, most of them only think they do and would quickly develop an aversion to heated battle once exposed to it.

Currently, governments purchase weapons with taxpayer's money. They purchase weapons for a professional military whose soldiers are mostly young adults from poor families—for the most part, young adults that couldn't catch a break in other avenues in life. This tends to breed an uncaring and/or disconnected attitude to war on the part of a great number of those that are funding it.

Members of a society must be encouraged to purchase their own means of self defense with their own money and then train in combat and martial arts on their own time. In fact, being armed for and trained in combat must be a part of the criteria for citizenship rank, at least for the male population. Not only will people such as this constitute a populace that is virtually immune to being conquered, it will create a culture of men able to defend themselves, their families and the neighborhoods.

Responsibility must be accompanied by the means and abilities to carry out the duties of that responsibility.

Food Services & Infrastructure

Public projects to increase the local availability of fresh, whole foods are essential. Livestock should be kept and produce grown by families where possible. People must be encouraged to attend to their own food supply as much as is practical.

No social subsidies of any kind should be placed on any food items. If people insist on packing themselves into tight residential areas, then they must confront the costs that this incurs. People must learn to pay the actual price of what they consume. It is a convoluted notion to pay taxes to a governmental body who then subsidizes the industries from which you acquire food products. If people directly paid for exactly what they were consuming, people's overall cost of living would not only be less since they aren't paying the fat-cat middlemen politicians in the federal government to doll out financial resources, but they would be paying no more and no less than their own fair share of the cost of their lifestyle. To take extreme ends of the spectrum, a vegetarian who grows most of his own food on his own property is still paying the same proportion of taxes to fund subsidies used to feed cattle as a man who eats two pounds of beef per day. Not really fair, is it?

People that cannot feed themselves are vulnerable. This point can't be stressed too much. A nation of people can be brought to its knees in a heartbeat if their food supplies are compromised. Vast populations are currently subject to the whim of those that can manipulate food costs and supplies. Dangerous indeed.

Infrastructure can be implemented to aid families and local communities in attending to the bulk of their own food requirements. Well-organized and sensible local cooperatives tending to the trade and distribution of locally raised and grown food is crucial. Ideally, each family should be producing enough food to sustain itself on their own property, even if service providers are tending to the actual work. They can still buy and sell food to add variety to their diet, but they should be able to take care of themselves in a pinch. If local societies can secure their own food production, they are rendered so much more powerful simply by way of the fact that they cannot be threatened and manipulated through their food and the withholding thereof. As such, self-sustainability with regard to food must also be a qualifying factor in citizenship ranks.

Furthermore, with local production, the quality of food can be readily ascertained and guaranteed. It will be fresher and the cost of transportation will be greatly reduced.

Families and their food supply should never be at the mercy of distant industries, covert influences and vulnerable supply lines. There is no need for food shortages of any kind. People just need to know what to eat, how to grow and raise it, and then be encouraged to do so in abundance.

Real Property Transaction

Selling property at price higher than the purchase price can only be done on the basis of contribution to, and development of, that property. If a man develops or improves land, he earns the right to sell it for what he invested into it. Untouched, undeveloped land cannot be bought or sold since no value can be assigned to it without investment of time into it. Laying claim to the right to sell virgin territory is mere opportunism — profit without production.

Paying rent on a piece of real estate gradually transfers ownership of that real estate into the hands of the tenant under a lease-to-own agreement. If and when the tenant has paid a sum of rent totaling the value of the property, they will have earned full ownership of that property.

The landowners win because they are rewarded with a share of the social investment fund for providing a home or place of business for another. This is their reward for being economic investors. Investment in real estate is vital so it is important to award real estate investors with a share of new money entering the economy. Furthermore, they secure passive income from the lease payments until the property is paid off.

The tenants win because they eventually earn full ownership of leased property, interest free. It sure beats paying the mortgage payments for their landlord as renters or, if they buy their own home, paying for their real estate two or three times over throughout the life of the mortgages.

Entitlement to the use of undeveloped land is awarded on the basis of reasonable claim and citizenship rank. Where someone has a reasonable claim to putting the land to good use or where it has been used by his family or associates but without development, they may make first claim. Where all other matters are equal, the issue is decided according to citizenship rank.

Technological Development

For technological development to flourish, for the culture to evolve, incentives for developing new technology must be allowed while preventing the monopolization of those developments.

Patents promote monopolies on technology and suppression of developments and can dearly hurt the expansion of the society and culture at large.

The policy of Social Viability is such that if someone develops new technology, anyone else may employ it in their own enterprise without restriction.

However, they must pay the inventor or developer what is due. There must still remain remuneration to the very valuable developers of new technologies.

An invention or development must be treated as a multiple consumer product (MCP). The time spent on the project of invention or development, the consumables used up and the equipment used would, together, constitute the production cost. The median consumption would consist of the median number of different business interests that utilize any given invention or development of that type. This provides a way to remunerate those that make breakthroughs for all of us.

For example, a person spends a total of 3000 man-hours (₮125) and outlays ₮25 in equipment costs and consumables in the invention of a propulsion device for vehicles. (There would be no substance component to the price since it is intellectual property.) If a median number of 50 different business interests utilize any given industrial invention or development, the price calculation would look like this:

Value Component	Amount
Labor	ŧ125
Substance	ŧ0
Materiel	ŧ25
Production Cost:	ŧ150
Median Consumption	ŧ50
Consumption Price:	ŧ3

In this case, each business that uses this invention in the production of some other product would owe the inventor ŧ3. The more the widespread the use of the invention, the more handsomely paid the inventor.

Furthermore, the inventor or developer of a technology that is utilized by others is given a special rank of citizenship which grants top priority in applications for loaned credit. This rank is designed to award those that develop society's capabilities and culture with further opportunity to do so.

As such, development is encouraged and stultification through monopolization is prevented.

CHAPTER 6
THE MESSENGER

THE PROBLEM: NEWS MEDIA & EDUCATION SYSTEMS

The Owners of Information

A LL CONSCIOUS action and opinion is based in, and dependent upon, decision. With the exception of instinctive reflex action, one doesn't act without prior decision on how to act. One cannot form an opinion about something without first deciding that something has or doesn't have certain qualities, which in turn are based on earlier decisions about the values that define those qualities. The decisions of people steer the course of history.

Decision is based upon information. People take information, notice similarities and differences between various data and conclude with a decision. Without information, no meaningful decision can occur. Furthermore, the information that is available dictates what conclusions can be drawn. Note well: the information available doesn't necessarily dictate exactly what particular conclusions are drawn; the information available dictates what conclusions *can* be drawn. False, inaccurate or misrepresented information perverts decisions by limiting the conclusions that can be drawn to incorrect ones. And that is the key element of effective propaganda. Propaganda is effective to the degree that it allows for a narrow scope of conclusions to be drawn from it.

For example, if someone had never personally encountered an automobile and the totality of information that they were given about motor cars was that they consumed natural resources, polluted the air, cost a lot of money to buy and maintain, were involved in the accidental deaths of vast numbers of people every year, and killed innumerable wild and domestic animals by running over them, the decision reached by any rational mind would be that cars are harmful and should not be used. It is not until one adds the vitally significant information that our vehicles allow people and goods to rapidly travel over long distances before the decision can be reached that they are worth having and using. By omitting this final positive datum, the conclusions reached can be limited to incorrect ones.

And so we get a glimpse of the power that the world's news and entertainment media wield. The information provided by the media shapes our decisions by manipulating information. Only the especially curious and questioning minds bother to probe and investigate using alternative sources of information. And these are the only minds that will ever reach any conclusions that do not fall within the dictates of the popular propaganda.

The ultimate enslavement is a voluntary bondage whereby the slaves wish for and invite subjugation. Thoroughly convince a slave that his condition is the best he can hope for—that he is lucky to be so well treated—and the slave will never rebel.

A society cannot function effectively in response to the enemies facing it when the information circulating is owned and formulated by the enemy.

Ignoring the fact that the media holdings are owned by corporate interests, which it will inevitably be faithful to, the media is paid by its advertisers—other related corporate interests. These advertising clients are the media outlets' bosses. If a pharmaceutical company invests large sums of money in television advertising, are the television networks going to run any exposés concerning the harmful and destructive nature of their drugs? Hardly. So, if it isn't the corporate owners of the media that ultimately own the public's perceptions and decisions, it is the same corporate owners through their advertising interests that do.

One of the more blatantly silly demonstrations of the deliberate propagandizing nature of the mass media is the news polls. A news poll that asks a question like, "Does Nation X possess weapons of mass destruction?" is obviously merely measuring the effectiveness of its propaganda. You will find that they will run such a poll after a week of news stories that claim, suggest and imply that Nation X is hiding stockpiles of WMDs. If they have found their propaganda successful, they will use the results to further their campaign by saying, "Look! 85% of Americans believe Nation X possesses weapons of mass destruction." Imagine a person telling you, "Bob is bad. Bob is bad. Bob is bad. Bob is bad." And then, "Is Bob bad, do you think?" News polls are nothing more than surveys that measure how well their message is sinking in. How would any average American have any slightest clue about some far-off nation's weapons stockpiles? They wouldn't, except through what they are told by news organizations. The only variable is how much the news consumers swallow the story.

The economy that you and I pay for is funding a mass propaganda campaign that is targeted at ourselves and our children. We are paying a lot of money for our own perverted brainwashing.

Fear Mongering

When something strikes fear or shock into a person, the person usually reacts with fixed attention centered on the source of that fear and shock. It is basic survival instinct. When a threat is perceived, it is valid human nature to give it priority attention so that the threat may be monitored. Being social creatures, we experience a similar fixation of attention when another is in peril of some kind or another.

The propaganda media use this basic human nature to manipulate us. They continually splash alarming images, sounds and messages past our senses and know that doing so will bring us back to watch or read or listen again tomorrow. In fact, the news and entertainment media have made an art form out of shocking people and it plays a very large part in keeping people coming back for more news and entertainment consumption.

The social and cultural impact of the fear mongering of the corporate media is immeasurable. This noxious practice will tend to drag people into a state of mild chronic hysteria that causes them to lose sight of the productive and healthy activities that promote the very safety and security they are alarmed about.

Closely related to the fear mongering is the sexual tantalization that is often used in covert and debased ways to usurp our attention. Reproduction is a strong natural urge, especially in younger people, and to use that urge to sell goods and make profit is perverted. It is so widely in practice that it has become acceptable, but it is quite deplorable to treat people like donkeys by luring them around with carrots. Like a gold-digging hussy that seduces rich old men, the industries that use such covert tactics to manipulate people are a sad reflection on our culture.

News as Entertainment

When news outlets are depended upon to make money for their owners and advertisers, they become quite frantic about making sure that people are attracted to them for news. Thus, their primary goal becomes making their news entertaining, rather than accurate, factual or socially constructive.

Keep in mind that the vast majority of people rely on mainstream news outlets to inform them of social affairs. Even the smallest distortions can and do result in massive departures in public perception of events from the real-world actuality. This is devastating for the general social sanity. Just as a person is sane to the degree that he can accurately perceive and understand his environment, so too is a society sane to the degree that its general population can accurately perceive and understand the social influences at work. Distorted information naturally leads to distorted perception and, in turn, causes departures in reason from what is logical and rational. This inevitably triggers social decay and disorder.

When news becomes a frantic effort to entertain you, there is very little regard for honest adherence to the truth— there is no business interest in doing so. And you better believe that big business worships only one god: Profit. Reality itself becomes fiction and life becomes a delusion that sucks vitality from our society at large.

Stultifying Education

For a child to be made to endure twelve full years of school in order to gain a regular education before entering the work force is onerous, to say the least. Parents and educators really should not wonder why their teens become rebellious whilst being forced to endure these painfully slow institutions. Schools run at the pace of the old men and women who run them; not at the pace of the energetic young students being instructed.

Using anything resembling a workable system of education, not even the slowest student will take twelve years of full-time study to learn enough to enter the work force, much less an added four years of college on top of that—even more in some cases!

First of all, children begin their education too late. Just because babies and small children cannot speak fluently, this does not mean they are unable to begin their education. Babies begin learning about their environment before they have even left the womb. Yet, parents are too often inclined to let the organized education of their children wait until they start school. These babies and little toddlers are so eager to learn about their environment, yet they are given inane toys and kept occupied with pointless "play" when all they want to do is to learn how to communicate and learn how to get along in the world. Again, parents wonder why toddlers often go through the "terrible twos and threes" when they have been putting them in play pens and doing their very best to keep the child occupied and out of their hair, rather than spending time with the child, showing them how the world works. Babies and children most want to learn. Take a baby or toddler (that is not hungry or tired) and point out things and name them, explain simple things to them. They will normally be very interested in what you are showing them. People in general are most happy and fulfilled when really learning—not robotically going to school— but really and successfully learning about something interesting and useful. And babies and small children are no different—more so, if anything.

Concerning the schooling system itself, the notion of putting groups of students together and making them all learn at the same rate is quite unworkable. The more apt students come to detest school for its tediousness and structure. If the class progresses at a faster rate, the least apt students get left behind and don't learn the material at all. Then, these slower students come to detest school because it is a frustrating and confusing waste of their time.

Also, the entire object of schools is to have students pass exams. This is not learning. This is memorization. To get students to cram data into their heads so as to regurgitate them during an exam—regardless of whether they truly grasp and understand it—is a waste of time. They will pass or not pass the test, get a grade on a piece of paper, and that is that. The memorized data often has no further bearing on their lives or careers.

Lastly, children are kept out of the workforce far too long. Most children aged twelve are emotionally developed enough to begin earning a living and they should not be kept from doing so. They should never be exploited—and neither should adults for that matter—but they should be given the opportunity and paid the same amount of money as an adult if they perform the same work.

For the most part, higher education should be carried out in conjunction with occupation in that field of work from the very beginning of the study in that field. There is no need to suspend earning a living to attend classes covering a vast plethora of extraneous material so that one can lay claim to some vague quality of being "properly educated." One becomes educated so much more by participating in a productive activity than by sitting in a classroom reading a text book or listening to a lecturer.

Completely aside from the social crime of public schools and universities being used as propaganda machines, the years of lost productivity, independence, and self-sufficiency have the effect of choking individual and social advancement as well as imposing years of idleness on young people who turn to juvenile delinquency to entertain themselves, causing untold distraction and disruption. We could be doing so much better.

Research Organizations & Think-Tanks

Few more crazy institutions exist than the research organizations and think-tanks that lurk in the shadows of our society. These thinly veiled manufacturers of reality are a disturbing element in our culture.

The news-media's treatment of events is blatantly fraudulent. This is no secret. Most are aware, at least to some degree, that media "spin" is injected into the information we absorb and, even though many don't quite grasp the significance of it or see any way to escape its influence, it is plainly there in everyone's face.

However, when research organizations launch charitable drives to "fight cancer" or some such cause, the deception is more obscure. Many are subtly drawn into false conclusions by implication. People are given the impression that mankind is yet to find a solution to these problems.

Taking cancer research as an example, there is a vast wealth of stories about people who have cured their cancer with simple yet powerful methods that do not involve any of the therapy or treatments of traditional medicine. These stories make it patently obvious that cancer is very curable and if independent people can turn to alternative solutions and handle conditions which our "experts" are completely unable to do, then our established medical profession and research organizations are dropping the ball to a criminally negligent degree. Yet donations keep pouring into cancer research and other things of the sort. These independent folks that cured their own cancer didn't need elaborate research labs to discover the plain logical sense that led them to handle their conditions. This fact coupled with the sheer lack of results that the research yields should raise red flags.

These research efforts do only two things, neither of which are useful or honorable. One, they funnel away a lot of money into their "research." What they actually research with all of those grants and donations is anyone's guess. Two, they promote the idea that certain problems are very complex and are unsolved, and that the solutions are beyond the common persons means because, "How could you possibly solve this problem if highly trained (and highly paid) experts haven't found the solution yet?" The fact is that solving problems is not in their financial interest since if they did, they would no longer have a cause for people to donate their hard-earned money to. Why present a solution and then have to spend years and millions hyping up some other threat to the collective survival?

And then we have these nebulous think-tanks that have the same function with regard to social and political issues. They study foreign policy, geopolitical issues and any other extravagant sounding so-called social science or application that seeks to obscure the truth by its very nature. The existence and function of these institutions again serve to create the apparency that there is some problem to solve and then pretend to try and solve it. The influences which govern social affairs are actually quite simple when all of the obfuscation is stripped away — obfuscation that these organizations erect in an attempt to justify their own sordid function.

Super-wealthy puppet masters get to pour tax-shelter donations into these movements which use these funds to hire self-proclaimed intellectuals to study false problems, creating an atmosphere that obscures their own influence. It works out very nicely for them and creates a world of incomprehensibility for the rest of us, whereby our economy has its lifeblood sucked upon by yet another parasite that, in turn, injects poison into the social blood supply to promote further decadence among our ranks.

THE SOLUTION: VIABLE INFORMATION POLICY

The Responsibility of the Messenger

Reporting news and, indeed, relaying information of any kind can, and often does, have a profound effect on subsequent events. In addition to such flagrant perpetrations of mistruth and propaganda, there are other more subtle and often more powerful manipulations that can and are used in the passing on of information.

This is an important subject; one that must be managed with due diligence if a society is to subsist peacefully and prosperously.

Responsibility for information disseminated must be taken by the disseminators of that information. To permit otherwise allows organizations and individuals to spread propaganda, hate and lies at will without concern for repercussion. Freedom of speech is quite necessary, but it must be accompanied by responsibility for what you say. Allowing reporters to spew any kind of garbage with merely a claim to quoting anonymous sources is as good as an open invitation for them to make up the news as they please.

If a journalist gives a platform to a lying, warmongering politician he must be as culpable as the politician for any harm that results from the lies being broadcast. Yes, it is the politician that spews forth the ill will, but it is the journalist that broadcasts it. They are both essential elements in the process and, as such, both must be held fully responsible for the consequences of their actions.

A bullet by itself is harmless. An unloaded firearm by itself is harmless. But combined they may wreak havoc and destroy lives. This is to say that to give pardon to the journalist under the specious excuse of free speech, no matter what venomous rot he or she disseminates, is to ignore the fact that a gun is needed to fire a bullet.

Let's juxtapose two scenarios illustrating what can be done with information as demonstration of how damaging the messenger can be.

Scenario one: A neighbor notices that the woman next door is cheating on her husband. He waits for the husband to come home, invites him to a bar to drink, gets him quite drunk and then proceeds to tell the husband with disgust and disdain of his wife's infidelity, adding suppositions about what the adulterers did behind closed doors and subtle suggestions about what the husband should do about it. The husband goes off and, in a drunken rage, murders his wife and her lover.

Scenario two: A neighbor notices that the woman next door is cheating on her husband. The neighbor confronts both the adulterers the next time he sees them slinking about together and asks them what the heck they think they're doing and reminds them of the despicable nature of their actions and demands that they handle the matter with integrity and honor. The wife-stealer shamefully leaves and does not return. The wife, heavy with guilt and remorse confesses to her husband and brings about a peaceful, if emotional, resolution to the issue.

Such juxtaposition helps to demonstrate how influential and responsible messengers can be in the outcome of events.

People must be held to account for their actions in relaying the information that they do—and don't—pass on, including the tone and manner in which they do it. Evidence must be convincing, but if a person or organization is found to have incited and encouraged criminal activity, that person must be subject to the same penalties as the actual perpetrators.

The most dangerous criminals in society use information—and the twisting thereof—to incite violence and mayhem in which they take no direct part. If instigators are ignored and direct perpetrators are the only ones brought to justice, the most dangerous and insidious criminals that lurk in the background are given free rein. This is a matter which, if ignored, can destroy civilizations and cultures.

It will not do to place mindless restrictions upon communication media and mechanisms in order to try and prevent such criminal acts. These kinds of restrictions cannot be viably implemented without hampering the vast majority of benevolent people and organizations in their communications. Justice must simply be done when harm is committed. Whether that harm is perpetrated with a gun or with lies whispered into the ear of the shooter, all criminals must be held accountable.

Application-Based Learning

As early as you can, teach your children how to communicate with the spoken word, with the written word, and with mathematical symbols. As early as you can, show them how to get around and function in society. And then let them learn a task and let them work. They will have the purpose, independence and self-respect that they thirst for and the society will be all the better for their contribution.

Children are happy learning. Children are happy helping. Children are happy exercising and moving about. Let them. Protect them, care for them and nurture them, but do not smother and restrict them. Give them the opportunity to develop and learn. If they get some scraped knees and smash some breakables along the way, they'll learn quickly not to fall or drop things. The learning experience will be far more valuable than the antiseptic to clean the scrape or the breakable that is smashed. They will learn skills by doing things. Skills learned will give them abilities, and abilities will allow them the opportunity for success that will generate high morale and productive happiness.

When they have developed to a point of being able to work in a job requiring minimal skill, let them work, let them discover what is out there and let them decide if they wish to enter a more highly skilled trade or profession. If they do, let them work and study further subjects in the pursuit of that occupation.

Unless they show a real interest in the subject, don't bother to teach advanced algebra to a child before they have any desire to become an engineer. If they wish to be a musician or an athlete, it will be a waste of their time and yours. Furthermore, it will be an onerous task since the child will see little point in learning the complex math and you will need to use strict discipline and duress—an excellent way to repel a child from a wish to learn such things.

Teach your children yourself. Do not send them to a school unless you must. Your child's ability to succeed in their lives is one of life's most gratifying and important products. Take responsibility for it.

It is firm policy in Social Viability to promote home-schooling-style infrastructure—to promote making curricula and materials available to parents so that they may teach their children themselves. In situations where schools are necessary, they are to be operated on a different basis altogether from what we are familiar with today. They will teach children according to a curriculum that each individual child covers at their own pace independent of how other children progress. They will have a list of materials to cover and practical projects to complete and they can complete it at their own pace. The teachers will be there to simply help the students learn their material, wherever they may be in their studies. If a child misses a class, or a week of classes, or even a year of classes, it will not matter. When they return to school they will pick up where they left off. They will follow their own course through a curriculum that uses materials, rather than teachers, to convey the theory of the subjects. The teachers will simply aid the children in their studies when they require it.

Teach our children as much as they will learn as quickly as they will learn it and let them take their place in society as soon as they reach for it. Families and societies will be all the stronger for the increased contribution, happier for the increased participation, and wiser for the increased responsibility.

Industry-Based Research & Development

Where you see research organizations conducting research concerning some perceived problem and the research goes on and on and on without any effective results, you are looking at an ulterior motive that is following less than productive purposes, at best. More likely, it is corrupt and devious.

Where you see research and development conducted by an individual or enterprise in the field in which they do business, making advances and developing new products, you see a drive to attain a specific result, and if the result is not attained within reasonable expense limits, it is abandoned. This is research with productive motive.

Research and development should be conducted in an industry-based manner, which is to say that it should be carried out by those in business in the particular field under research and development, or by those seeking to do business in that field. There is no place in the social organizational structure for research organizations that beg for grants and donations to do research, making the conducting of research an end unto itself, completely independent of the usefulness of any developments derived. An industry devoted to research and development as its own product is a sham industry.

If research is worth doing, it has a productive business interest involved. If powerful industrial enterprises neglect to undertake research and development to expand their operations, their foolish neglect will open the door to smaller businesses and private inventors to make technological breakthroughs and capitalize on those advances.

Industry should also be encouraged to enter the endeavor of higher learning. It is far more efficient for specialized industry to teach specialized skills to students with productive facilities than for universities or colleges to purchase very expensive equipment for the sole purpose of instruction. Such an arrangement not only opens up the additional business of instruction for the industrial companies, it provides a much more smooth transition from instruction to production and inevitably leads to greater productivity for the entire society.

I realize that with industrial instruction, we may miss the opportunity for the socialistic mass-indoctrination that occurs when we herd all of our young minds onto giant college campuses, but I guess that's just one more degenerative social institution we'll have to do without.

CHAPTER 7
OPPORTUNITY

THE PROBLEM: ACCELERATED DEGENERATION

Abandoning Self-Determinism

TOO MANY are failing to identify the enemy. Too many are happy with the addictive, degenerative habits being offered up to them. Like the junkie that keeps buying drugs from an insistent dealer because it seems easier to do so than to fight the addiction and the corruptive influence, Western society at large continues to consume the cultural crack being offered up to it.

And, like the junkie, those buying into the decaying culture know in the back of their minds that they are sinking deeper into a trap of personal and social corruption. "If it is on television, it must be acceptable," seems to be an all-too-common mentality that allows personal responsibility and integrity to be sacrificed to the god of popularity.

Abandon self-determinism, have your identity and lifestyle spoon-fed to you, be responsible for as little as possible and you will help enormously to exert pressure on the throttle that is driving our culture's accelerated degeneration.

Using Banks & Inflated Currencies

The central banks of the world have established currencies and a multitude of member banks that deal in their currencies.

When you use their money, you subject yourself to the invisible tax—the covert robbery—that is inflation. They are devaluing the money for their own profit as it sits in your wallet.

When you use their money, you are at the mercy of their member banks when you need a loan. You must pay usurious interest on your mortgage and then home insurance on top of that. Most pay for their homes two or three times before they own it, not counting the insurance premiums. All because we use their money.

When you keep your savings in one of their banks, they use your money as their commodity, trading with it and leveraging it to their hearts content. They use your money to destabilize and subvert the economy of your society.

Our societies are slaves to the banking system because— and *only* because—we use the money that they offer up to us.

Every time you take out a loan or conduct a transaction using their money, you feed fuel to the engine that is powering your society's accelerated degeneration.

Granting Power to the Politicians

The corrupt political system and the morally compromised puppet-politicians only dictate to us because we bestow upon them their power. We voluntarily grant them license to impose war-mongering, economically retarded, and culturally depraved measures that undermine all that we strive to establish for ourselves and our families.

When people scramble out to the polls on Election Day to vote for their favorite political actor, they are supporting the dysfunctional electoral system and, thus, validating the position of the winner of the apparent election. Even if the election is not a fixed charade, any legitimate winner of import is almost always owned by those that almost never have the public's best interests at heart. Any politician that swings any significant weight at all is either bought or buried.

If your car wears a bumper sticker that supports any political candidate; if you participate in any political polling; if you hold any party affiliation; if you waste an hour to submit a vote in an election, you grant power to those in office. And it has been a long time indeed since a truly noble statesman took high office anywhere in the Western world and made significant strides for civilization.

To lend credence to the political process and the criminals it spawns by voting or playing along with the political process in any way does little more than help to steer the course of accelerated degeneration for our culture.

Feeding the Justice System

As long as people are willing to use law suits to extract money out of others, justice and responsibility will remain independent and disconnected from one another. Bright young people will continue to be drawn into the legal profession in pursuit of wealth, only to have their talent wasted in a system that perverts the concept of right and wrong.

As long as people are willing to break the law in an effort to compensate for being oppressed by economic tyranny, the criminal courts and prison systems will get richer. Backward and repressive laws provide every justification to break the law, but to take the bait and commit crimes is to play right into the hands of the forces that seek to enslave. Despite any provocation that may be, do not resort to criminality to make your way. There are ways to better your lot legitimately and honorably. Do not run afoul of the law and degrade yourself with dishonesty and pointless rebellion.

To run afoul of the law or to play opportunistic games in civil suits is to provide ever improving traction for the accelerated degeneration that we all need to avert.

Doing Business with Criminals

Corrupt corporations are able to pervert our economic environment because we do business with them. Yes, many of the big players draw funding through government contracts, as in the case of arms manufacturing, but you are still doing business with them via the government with whom you do business. These sectors which thrive off the federal government's tax revenue still coexist with consumer-based corporations in an economic web that is woven by the elite finance community. And like any interlinked web, each part of it relies on all other parts to retain their integrity, for if one or two anchoring components fail, then the entire web begins to flap in the breeze and fails to function effectively.

When you do business with any corporation that constitutes this web, you feed the disease that plagues you. When you do business with any entity that operates on criminal principles, to that degree, you compromise your own moral integrity and rearrange your own guiding values. There are greedy businesses producing substandard, dangerous and poisonous products and services. Educate yourself and do not buy from them or hire them.

When you do business with these enemies of your prosperity, you merely put fuel in the tank that provides a reservoir of power for our collective accelerated degeneration.

Consuming Toxic Information

We do not need to hear about the various violent robberies, murders and rapes that happen around our cities. Having these images and pieces of information hanging on our minds as we go about our business does not make us safer or more able to protect ourselves. Being honest, alert, perceptive, and being highly competent in self-defense makes us safer and more able to protect ourselves.

We do not need to constantly hear about fatal car accidents. Learning of each of these tragedies does not make us safer on the road. Being competent and focused drivers is what makes traffic accidents less likely.

Consuming the news fed to you at face value corrupts your mental patterns and cripples your ability to be in control of your life. It is not this way by accident. Corrupt influences seek to foster dependencies in their consumers. Dependent consumers are less able, less creative, and more predictable— their return business can be counted on. Hence they seek to engage you in habit-forming practices. Modern marketing seems to revolve around this concept.

Even worse, our children are being indoctrinated into this at early ages, many watching atrocious amounts of television, being fed psychotropic drugs to modify behavior, and being taught backward information in backward ways. Not only are they being fed counterfeit data, it is being fed to them in a manner that makes it hard to learn. They aren't even being given a fighting chance to learn the wrong information that is presented to them! The blighting of intelligence and competence of future generations is possibly the greatest atrocity being committed in western culture today. It is one thing to plunder the prosperity of the current society, but to deliberately infect future chances at rehabilitation is blatantly evil.

If you passively consume mainstream news, accepting it at face value, or if you send your children to most modern schools and colleges, you are sabotaging the brakes that may halt the accelerated degeneration of our race.

THE SOLUTION: CREATIVE PROSPERITY

Decide to Change Conditions

Constructive, committed action must be preceded by a firm and clear decision. Your part in building a viable society that may survive the mess that the current culture is creating must include, as a prerequisite, the firm, conscious decision to be a part of the solution that upholds righteous integrity, fosters family values, and contributes loyally to noble organizations, enterprises and societies. This decision paves the way to a solution that gives man a fighting chance at economic and social viability.

Having made that decision, what next? What does one do about it? Step one: Register with Social Viability. You can do this at: **www.socialviability.com**. A membership with Social Viability will connect you to the social framework that uses this book as its founding policy.

Engage in Legitimate Trade

Modern living and social prosperity depend upon the viable function of its economic activity. The viability of an economy is one of the best indicators of cultural advancement and the primary factor that determines its general sustained standard of living.

Go to **www.exchangedynamics.net** and open an account. A membership with Social Viability is the only requirement. Use the Exchange Dynamics online marketplace to begin trading in Exchange Time wherever you can. As you trade in Exchange Time more and more you will be trading with the common corrupted money less and less. This will reduce the power of the existing corrupt social systems and, more importantly, it will help to build the movement that will restore viability to Western culture.

Find or Become a Worthy Leader

Having opened your Social Viability membership, placing yourself among those building a new society; having opened an account with Exchange Management, allowing you to interact economically; the next vital step is to get organized socially.

The activities of yourself and your friends who are building new standards for social viability will gain momentum as the scope of your activities grow. The only way to capitalize on that momentum and sustain it is to organize. If productive people carry out all of the functions of a modern society and interchange their goods and services effectively and equitably, they will grow and prosper provided they operate within a known and agreed upon social framework.

People have free wills, have unique ideas and will run off in different directions, solving problems in uncoordinated ways if no unifying factors exist. The framework of Social Viability organization gives everyone an agreed-upon set of policies to use in their social dealings. Good ideas will flourish in an environment that fosters such, and people will be able to solve problems in ways that do not sabotage others and, in fact, will help others solve the same problems with coordinated effort.

As Social Viability grows and as the need arises, organizations to administer social functions will be chartered and the necessary functions attended to.

Gather around wise leadership that follows the sound principles of Social Viability. If insufficient or inadequate leadership exists, step into that role and help direct the course of social activity.

Establish Social Dignity

Nothing will drive a population into a collective dementia more relentlessly than a system of laws and sentencing that is inconsistent, arbitrary and corrupt. People cannot be truly free while the specter of injustice hangs over them. People cannot have pride in a society that treats the underprivileged innocent with scorn and punishment while at the same time protecting privileged criminals from penalty for heinous acts.

The next vital step that must be taken to reassert viability to our societies is to restore honor and dignity to our culture. It is crucial to reward the productive and benevolent with support and unfettered service, and to penalize the criminal and malevolent with restrictions and revocations.

As the need arises, justice organizations will be founded and provide court administrators and civic arbiters to ensure such a state of appropriate social intercourse exists.

Use these systems, and if they don't exist, put them in place according to the policies of Social Viability. This vital step, when carried out with honest diligence, will act as the glue that holds together the organized functioning of the society.

Exercise Discretion

Do business with those enterprises, organizations and institutions that demonstrate integrity, effective benevolence and balanced social responsibility. Be questioning, curious and interested in the dealings of those you deal with. Your society is yours to be responsible for.

Do not be lazy in identifying the influences in your environment. Do not robotically accept what you are told about who is who and what is what. Go out and look. Who is productive? Who is being effective in improving conditions in society? If you can't directly look, take in an array of observations and evaluate carefully according to fundamental principles, always keeping in mind the interests of the purveyors of information as you digest their views.

Your decisions help steer the energies of society. Your discretion is needed to help drive those energies into the areas that will foster civilization and social prosperity for us all.

Fertilize Minds

Inoculate yourself against the mainstream news. Actively seek alternative news sources and viewpoints that make real sense of current events and that show the mainstream news for what it really is—a propaganda campaign.

When you consume mainstream news, view it with a critical eye and identify the interests that are served by the messages being fed to you. Watch and listen, but don't get suckered in.

Find sources of news that provide useful, pertinent data as opposed to the traffic reports, celebrity scandals, political babble and the latest bloody murder. Seek out sources that are worth paying for and pay subscriptions for them so that interests other than your own aren't paying for them.

Know what is happening by looking, investigating and researching; not by merely listening passively to the information fed to you. There is an important maxim here: any information, advice or assistance offered is offered on the terms of the person presenting that information, advice or assistance. It has been collected and processed through their eyes according to their interests and delivered in keeping with their priorities. Information, advice or assistance that you acquire through your own active pursuit is garnered on your own terms, processed through your own eyes with your interests in mind, and in step with your priorities. What is relevant and important for another may not be for you, and vice versa.

Next, educate your children—yourself. Do not leave such an important task to a stranger or a state system that sanctions the drugging of children. Don't have the time? Don't have the money? The reason Social Viability exists is so that families may make the time to do such things. Economic constraints are tight for many. That equates to money and time being at a premium. Avail yourself of the vital steps contained herein and you will find relief.

With that relief, comes opportunity. And opportunity is what Social Viability is all about.

෨෮

www.ingramcontent.com/pod-product-compliance
Lightning Source LLC
Chambersburg PA
CBHW031930190326
41519CB00007B/481